P&O CRUISES

BRITANNIA

Inspired by the past. Designed for the future.

Brian D. Smith

Ferry Publications

Published by: Ferry Publications, PO Box 33, Ramsey, Isle of Man IM99 4LP

Tel: +44 (0) 1624 898445   Fax: +44 (0) 1624 898449   E-mail: ferrypubs@manx.net   Website: www.ferrypubs.co.uk

Title page: A proud moment indeed for P&O Cruises as their new flagship arrives at her home port for the very first time. (James Morgan)

*Below: Seen at the completion of her delivery voyage from her Italian builders, the **Britannia** is welcomed to her new home in the traditional fashion. (P&O Cruises)*

CONTENTS

Produced and designed by Ferry Publications trading as Lily Publications Ltd

PO Box 33, Ramsey, Isle of Man, British Isles, IM99 4LP

Tel: +44 (0) 1624 898446   Fax: +44 (0) 1624 898449

www.ferrypubs.co.uk   e-mail: info@lilypublications.co.uk

Printed and bound by Printer Trento © Lily Publications 2016

First Published: January 2016

FOREWORD

BY DAVID DINGLE, CHAIRMAN, CARNIVAL UK

Britannia is a most fitting name for the largest and most innovative cruise ship built for Britain. She is the newest addition to the P&O Cruises fleet, which, with its long and famous heritage, remains Britain's favourite cruise line. Named by Her Majesty the Queen in a prestigious ceremony here in Southampton, the cruise capital of the United Kingdom, *Britannia* expresses the contemporary spirit of P&O Cruises and captures the spirit of today's Britain, a place of renewed style and sophistication, of optimism and excitement. Reflecting this, the *Britannia* marks a new era of growth and success for the cruise industry.

With the introduction of *Britannia*, P&O Cruises has underpinned its unique commitment to building ships specifically designed to anticipate the tastes of today's British cruise passenger. She is a modern classic, a ship for current and future generations, offering authentic travel by sea in an enduringly contemporary setting. She is the bench mark by which other ships will be judged and undoubtedly countless passengers will enjoy a ship brimming with character and innovation whilst collecting many happy memories that will last for a lifetime.

One of my great pleasures, and indeed privileges as Chairman of our wonderful Company, is to travel on the *Britannia* and observe our passengers having such a fabulous time on this magnificent vessel which even now has earned her place as part of P&O Cruises proud history. I hope you all enjoy reading Brian Smith's new book which gives a unique insight into the design and construction of this, the largest ship ever built to serve the British cruise market.

David Dingle. (P&O Cruises)

INTRODUCTION

BY CHRISTOPHER EDGINGTON VP, MARKETING – P&O CRUISES

When P&O founders Arthur Anderson, Brodie McGhie Wilcox and Captain Richard Bourne first imagined ocean travel in 1837, little did they know they had discovered the rarest commodity known to modern man; time. Early travel on their mail ships to exotic ports via postal routes began as an affordable way for people to see the world, but the trio had unwittingly hit upon a ground-breaking concept, and the leisurely pace of life at sea struck a chord with adventurous Brits.

Not only was P&O credited with revolutionising the way people travelled by sea but it was also persuading the rest of the world that the future of the maritime industry would depend on companies replacing its aging fleet of sailing ships with newer steam-powered vessels.

Today, P&O Cruises is again leading the way with the introduction of the *Britannia*, the biggest ship designed exclusively for Britain. A "modern classic", the *Britannia* heralds a new era of holiday choice that no one else can offer, combining classic signatures honed over the course of our history with a host of new features designed with one eye firmly on the future. Chief amongst these features are her restaurants, bars and cafes, offering a tongue-tingling array of menus and culinary experiences created by P&O Cruises very own 'Food Heroes'; James Martin, Marco Pierre White, Atul Kochhar, Eric Lanlard, wine expert Olly Smith and cheese expert Charlie Turnbull.

In a first for the fleet, these celebrity chefs and experts will share their skills and knowledge with our passengers in The Cookery Club, a 24-person state-of-the-art cookery school. Joining them will be other culinary colossi including Mary Berry CBE, Pierre Koffmann, Paul Rankin and Commendatore Antonio Carluccio OBE.

However, the *Britannia*'s most outstanding design statement is reserved for her three-deck high atrium with illuminating 'Star Burst' sculpture; offering that spectacular wow that every ship strives for. Not content with impressing her passengers with the culinary delights that P&O Cruises is so famous for, the *Britannia* also provides the largest British spa at sea, a cutting-edge theatre with LED wall, four pools, gym,

Christopher Edgington. (P&O Cruises)

and a multi-million pound art collection including a specially commissioned representation of the 'Spirit of Modern Britain' from artist Johnny Bull.

Combine these facilities with a superb range of accommodation, outstanding children's facilities and a range of other innovative features all designed to give you the perfect cruise experience, and it's easy to see why everyone is talking about *Britannia*.

Beautifully illustrated with photographs from respected marine photographers as well as P&O Cruises own heritage collection, this book will be a welcome collection to both the maritime enthusiast as well as the many people who want a fabulous souvenir of their holiday on the flagship of Britain's favourite cruise company.

Run away to sea!

BRITANNIA

The History of P&O

P&O
WORLD WIDE SERVICES

Today, P&O Cruises is a very successful British cruise brand operating eight ships, all dedicated to the British cruise market and sailing to various locations all around the world. They have a proud and interesting history which can be traced back to the early 19th century when in 1815 Brodie McGhie Willcox started trading as a shipbroker in a small office, close to the River Thames in the centre of London. Not a great deal is known about how well Willcox did in these early years but he clearly traded with some success as in 1822 he had the need to employ a young clerk from the Shetland Islands by the name of Arthur Anderson who had served with the Royal Navy during the Napoleonic Wars and therefore had some important maritime experience to add to the company. Such was Anderson's drive and enthusiasm that within three years of joining the company, Willcox decided to make him a partner and in 1825 the two of them started trading as Willcox and Anderson. Not only did they act as ship brokers, they actually became ship owners after a small American schooner had gone aground near Dover and her owners had wanted to sell the wreck to limit the liability of the damaged ship. Once Willcox and Anderson had purchased the vessel, they repaired her and fitted her with

legitimate Queen and once again backed the winning side. This was to be of great importance to the company in later years as the Spanish Ambassador to London would use great influence to help the company win new contracts to the Iberian Peninsula.

SAIL GIVES WAY TO STEAM

At this time there were a number of great and famous men who were starting shipping companies using steamships, including Isambard Kingdom Brunel who was running a single ship service across the Atlantic to New York with his latest ground-breaking vessel, the *Great Western*. The problem was that steamships were still in their infancy and were extremely unreliable. When ships broke down there was more often than not, nothing to replace them and Anderson quickly realised that for a shipping company to succeed it needed to have a fleet of vessels which included a spare ship ready to enter service if required. In 1834 they decided to rebrand their company with an eye to making it the premier company taking cargo and passengers to the Iberian Peninsula. A prospectus was issued with the company name of The Peninsular Steam Navigation Company, the Oriental suffix was added later

*In 1835 Willcox & Anderson chartered the 206 ton **William Fawcett** to open their first 'Peninsular Steam' service to Spain and Portugal. (Ferry Publications Library)*

some defensive armaments before sending her on her first journey for the company to Portugal carrying various cargos and a small number of passengers. The name of this ship is not known but it began a dynasty that continues today in the form of P&O Cruises.

During this period Portugal was involved in a civil war and Anderson began the very dangerous and risky business of gun running for the Portuguese Crown and its supporters, which included an elderly British Admiral by the name of Sir Charles Napier who later worked for Anderson. The decision proved to be a wise one as the Queen of Portugal won her war and rewarded Willcox and Anderson with contracts to serve her country from the UK. No sooner had the war in Portugal finished than a further civil war broke out in Spain. Again Willcox and Anderson sided with the

when they began to explore routes into the Mediterranean and across to Egypt.

In 1835, the Spanish Ambassador in London took steps to introduce the benefits of a reliable steamship service to Spain and chartered several steamships from the Dublin & London Steam Packet Company. He did not forget the involvement of Willcox and Anderson in supporting the Spanish Queen a few years before and so placed the management of this new venture under the Peninsular Steam Navigation Company.

To supplement this additional trade, the company purchased a 206-ton paddle steamer called the *William Fawcett* which had been built in Liverpool in 1828. With two large sails and twin paddle wheels, she had been named after the engineer who had built her engines and is regarded

Top: In this 1875 etching from The Graphic, the captain of P&O's **Sumatra** *is leading a Sunday religious service on deck as the steamer progresses through the Red Sea.*

Above: An etching from The Illustrated London News depicting the newly completed **Bentinck** *at anchor in the Thames prior to her maiden voyage for P&O.*

Right: The **Poonah** *at anchor in the Grand Canal at Venice, the first large steamer ever to visit the city. This etching from The Illustrated London News makes a fascinating comparison with the frontispiece view of the cruise ship* **Arcadia**.

(All Bruce Peter collection)

as being the first ship to be actually owned by the Peninsular Steam Navigation Company. To give some idea of comparisons, *William Fawcett* was less than 100 metres long and her engines had a total output of around 60 horse power. P&O Cruises latest ship, *Azura*, is almost 300 metres long, 120,000 gross tonnes and her engines have a total power output closer to 100,000 horse power.

By 1837 Willcox and Anderson owned a fleet of seven steamships which were all fitted with auxiliary sails whilst most ships at this time were sail ships with auxiliary steam engines. They had many competitors who were struggling to make their steamships pay but Anderson believed that if they could offer a regular service which would leave exactly when advertised and arrive at its destination at a designated time then people would be willing to pay the extra needed to make this service viable. It is important to remember that at this time, most services were dependent on the wind and tide and timetables were little more than a planner's dream. With the strong currents in the English Channel and the heavy seas of the Bay of Biscay it could take anything up to ten days for a ship to reach Portugal from London and on occasions even three weeks could be the norm.

A TIMETABLED SERVICE

Clearly matters had to improve and Anderson realised that if he could reduce these times and provide a reliable service then his new company was in with a chance of success. It was decided to advertise a sailing from Falmouth to Vigo in Spain that would take only 54 hours, an unbelievably quick time for the period. There would be a sailing connection to London which would take another two days but they were offering a real timetable from England to Spain which was significantly less than anyone else could ever hope to offer. Willcox was still worried about making such a business profitable but Anderson convinced him that if they could win another large contract delivering goods to the continent then the business would be a success. The suggestion came from Richard Bourne, one of the company's senior employees who had joined them in 1835 from the Dublin & London Steam Packet Company. Bourne convinced Willcox and Anderson that the way to make their new company profitable was to win the Royal Mail contract to Spain and Portugal. He believed that any company that took the Royal Mail across the sea always made a profit. The current contract to run the mail was up for renewal so Willcox immediately put plans together ready to tender the Admiralty when the contract was advertised. After many deliberations between the three executive figures of the Peninsular Steam Navigation Company, they managed to offer the Admiralty a fixed timetabled service for which they would charge the Government £30,000 per annum to take the Royal Mail to the Iberian Peninsula.

The Admiralty were reluctant to do business with the three men but Willcox, by now an MP, managed to convince the Government that they could do the job safely and reliably.

No one else could match the price or delivery times that Willcox and Anderson were offering so on 22nd August 1837, the new contract to carry the Royal Mail to Iberia was duly signed. This is now regarded as the official beginning of the company which today trades as P&O Cruises. On 1st September, the largest ship in the fleet, the 450-ton *Don Juan* left England bound for Spain carrying the first cargo belonging to the Royal Mail and on board were Anderson and his wife Mary Ann. The operation with the Royal Mail was so successful that within a year the Government asked the company to make plans for taking the mail from Gibraltar right through to Alexandria in Egypt. The importance of winning this contract could not be underestimated as the significance of Alexandria was not the mail or the trade to Egypt itself but the fact it was the next staging post for the lucrative mail run to India and the countries beyond the sub-continent.

TO THE ORIENT

The Suez Canal, linking the Mediterranean to the Red Sea, was still some time from being completed by the French and it was not until 1869 that it was open for traffic. In the 1830s it involved ships docking at Alexandria or Cairo before their passengers and cargo continued their journey across the Isthmus of Suez, a slow and sometimes dangerous desert journey of 150 miles on camel or donkey. One of the reasons that the British Government gave the Alexandria contract to the Peninsular Steam Navigation Company was that they promised to send the mail in modern steamers calling at British ports such as Gibraltar and Malta on the way. Others sent the mail partly across land and France in particular. There was never any evidence that the French authorities interfered with the British Mail but Britain had been at war with France for as long as anyone could remember and there were many members of the British Government who were not yet ready to trust the French with the British Royal Mail.

To take on this extra work the company needed additional ships and employees but before it could do this it required incorporation by Royal Charter which would basically grant the company limited status. It finally received this in December 1840 alongside a new set of directors with Willcox and Anderson remaining as Managing Directors. The name Oriental was officially added to the company's name and from this point on it was known as the Peninsular and Oriental Steam Navigation Company or, more affectionately as P&O for short. In exchange for shares, the company acquired a ship from a trans-Atlantic firm who had run into difficulties after one of its competitors, Samuel Cunard, had won the Atlantic Royal Mail contract. It is interesting to see that Richard Bourne was completely right in his prediction that any company than won the contract to carry the Royal Mail had a greater chance of success as today, be it in a significantly different form, the only two significant shipping companies that were trading in the 1830s and still survive in the 21st century are P&O Cruises and Cunard; both of whom had Royal Mail contracts from the British Government.

In the 1840s, the only company taking the Royal Mail to India was the powerful East India Company whose Royal Charter went right back to the times of Queen Elizabeth I. They controlled all the mail from Bombay to the UK and were not about to give up this very lucrative trade without a fight.

The terms of P&O's Charter were that it could take the mail to India but it did not state what part of India. Rather than cause friction with a registered heavy weight company with influential friends, P&O decided to send the Royal Mail to Calcutta. The problem with this was that most passengers wanted to go to Bombay, not Calcutta, and had been used to extremely lavish ships offering a great deal of comfort; be it that they were still powered by sail and very slow. To compete, P&O were going to have to build at least two new and very large, comfortable steamships that were capable of taking a combination of passengers and cargo to run between Suez and India. By running a steamship service so far from home P&O were coming up against a set of logistics that had never been encountered before.

In those days it was not just a question of bunkering in England, then setting sail and arriving in India a few weeks later as there were no established places to take on additional coal and provisions. Sailing ships carrying coal had to be dispatched in advance to various locations on the route to await the steamer where it would then refuel. The sailing ships would also carry agents to these locations where they would arrange to purchase fresh water, food and other provisions.

The new ships would cost £60,000 each and would be wooden paddle steamers of around 2,000 tons with a length of 240 feet. Each would have 60 cabins and berths for 150 people. They were elegant ships with three masts of sail and two funnels. They had clipper bows and wide stern windows. The normal arrangement for passenger ships of the time was to have the public rooms in the centre of the ship with the cabins at the forward and after ends. P&O decided to reverse this with large passenger rooms at the bow and stern and the cabins running in the middle of the ship, the idea being that in rough weather the centre of the ship tends to move around less and therefore when people were resting in their cabins they would have a more comfortable passage.

The first of the new ships, *Hindonstan*, sailed from Southampton for India on 24th September 1842 via Gibraltar, St Vincent, Ascension Island, Cape Town, Mauritius and Ceylon taking a total of 91 days. Upon her arrival she immediately set sail for Suez on what was to be her regular route via Madras, Ceylon and Aden. The second ship was named *Bentinck* and joined her sister in the following year. P&O could now take the Royal Mail and passengers from London to India using *Great Liverpool* or *Oriental* from England to Alexandria before everyone went across land to Suez where they would pick up one of the new ships on to India. The journey times were significantly shorter than those being offered by the East India Company who could still take up to a year to reach India, going around the Cape of Good Hope in South Africa.

GROWING THE PASSENGER TRADE

After winning the new mail contracts to India, Willcox and Anderson looked at new ways to increase the profitability of their company without the need for any additional expenditure. Anderson managed to convince Willcox that people would be willing to pay good money to travel on their steamships and to visit the many interesting ports and countries that P&O traded with. It was another imaginative idea which he had originally conceived back in 1835 when he ran a small newspaper in the Shetland Isles called the 'Shetland Journal'. In one particular issue there was empty advertising space which Anderson had been very keen to fill up by any means necessary. So he used it to advertise 'Ghost' cruises on local ships plying the waters around the Shetland Islands that didn't even exist.

However, it was not until 1844 that the first ever real cruise was advertised in the British press, sailing from England to the Mediterranean and such exotic destinations as Malta, Athens and Rhodes.

The novelist William Makepeace Thackeray was given a complimentary ticket by P&O on one of their first ever cruises as a way of obtaining free advertising for the new venture. He wrote the book 'Notes of a Journey from Cornhill to Grand Cairo' under the pseudonym of Michael Angelo Titmarsh and travelled on several ships, including the *Lady Mary Wood*, the *Tagus* and the *Iberia* to Gibraltar, Greece and Egypt, all of which were scheduled services rather than a leisurely cruise to those destinations. Thackeray was very grateful to P&O for their kindness and wrote very highly of them, if not the places that he visited but the strategy worked and P&O had their free publicity. P&O's network of Mediterranean and Black Sea routes continued to build in the 1840s, including a route to Constantinople. However, these were not as successful as the routes to India and the east so some of them were dropped in favour of the more lucrative Royal Mail services.

The start of the Crimean War in 1853 put a stop to any cruise trade that P&O had built up in the Mediterranean and although the war lasted less than 30 months, it was some considerable time before cruising was again considered by the company. In the meantime they continued to expand their services throughout the Indian Ocean and the Far East although this rapid expansion of ships and routes was to have its problems. For one thing the amount of coal which needed transporting to the ports where P&O ships were refuelling increased significantly. Every steamship on a trip to India needed three sailing colliers to sail ahead of it, making sure that there was enough coal for the ship to arrive at its destination. It was estimated that at any one time P&O had over 90,000 tons of coal stored around the world ready for their ships to use on its routes to and from Britain. P&O also had to feed up to 10,000 people per day at a time when there was no frozen food or refrigeration. Ships were going to sea with entire farmyards on board, all of which would have been eaten by the time the ship arrived at its destination. To help solve this problem P&O began building its own farms on land close to the ports where the ships refuelled. This way less livestock needed to be put on the ships in Britain, meaning there was more room to carry additional cargo and a plentiful supply of suitable meat was always available once the ship had sailed.

Other shipping companies were very jealous of the success of P&O and a Parliamentary enquiry into the company was held in 1852. This found no wrongdoing by the Board of Directors and upon its completion the company celebrated its findings by winning the Royal Mail contract to Australia. The East India Company could not compete with the new and expanding company and its services to India were deteriorating as they desperately tried to hang on to their mail contracts to Bombay. They were now vastly inferior to P&O when it came to reliability, timings and comfort.

In response, the East India Company subcontracted out some of its work carrying the Royal Mail and did so to less than reputable companies who on occasions lost the mail in transit. To obtain the Royal Mail run between London and Bombay it had secured subsidies from both the Indian and British Governments to the tune of over £105,000 a year at a time when P&O were waiting for the chance to outmanoeuvre the ailing company and take its trade. The

*Designed for naval service in time of war, **Australia** of 1892 and **Himalaya**, brought enhanced safety through her many hull divisions and also grand hotel-like interiors to the P&O fleet, in which she served for 12 years. (Bruce Peter collection)*

opportunity came after a gross act of complacency when the East India Company managed to lose an entire consignment of Royal Mail after it had arrived at Aden where there were none of the company ships to take it on to Bombay.

Rather than wait for one of their ships to arrive, the company decided to send it on to India in an Arab dhow which left Aden and was never seen again. Upon receiving news of this debacle, the P&O board immediately submitted to the British Government a set of proposals promising to deliver the Royal Mail to India using only its large modern steamers, stopping at only British-controlled ports and for a subsidy of only one-fifth of what the Government had been paying to the East India Company. The fate of the East India Company was sealed and P&O finally won the profitable Royal Mail run to Bombay.

Matters were progressing well for P&O and the future was looking very bright when the original founder of the company, Brodie McGhie Willcox died in a freak accident just outside Portsmouth in 1862. The co-founder and driving force Arthur Anderson died a few years later in 1868. At the time of their deaths the Peninsular and Oriental Steam Navigational Company had 51 steamships in service, more than any other shipping operator, and had expanded from a simple service to the Iberian Peninsula to a large multinational company serving the British Government and carrying hundreds of thousands of passengers to three continents. In 31 short years P&O had become one of the largest and most successful shipping companies the world had ever seen.

UNDER NEW LEADERSHIP

Anderson's choice as his successor as Chairman of P&O was a young Aberdonian called Thomas Southerland. He had joined the company when he was 18 and served at various levels on most of their trade routes. He had shown a drive and determination similar to that of Anderson himself and quickly demonstrated that he was a suitable replacement for the great man when he managed to open a new trade link to Japan when only the Dutch had been allowed to do business with what was then still a very closed and secret country. He returned to work at the company's headquarters in London and in 1872 was voted as P&O's new Managing Director at the very young age of only 38 years.

The Suez Canal had finally opened in 1869 and this caused P&O a few problems as new tonnage had to be built for the now direct service to India. The Government wanted to renegotiate its subsidiary for taking the Royal Mails as now it could be done much more efficiently and cheaply. As a result P&O saw its revenues drop at a time when its expenditures were rising; the opening of the Suez Canal was not a happy event for P&O's finances. However, the company persevered and by remaining true to its principles of offering large modern, comfortable ships, with a quick and reliable timetable, it soon overcame these adversities. This was best demonstrated in 1887 when Queen Victoria celebrated her Golden Jubilee and P&O marked the occasion by building four 6,000-ton 'Jubilee' ships, *Victoria, Britannia, Oceania* and *Arcadia*.

*The first duty for the newly delivered **Medina** was to perform the role of Royal Yacht, carrying King George V and Queen Mary to India for the Delhi Durbar in 1911. This pageant was a high point of the Raj. She too was torpedoed by a U-boat in February 1917 sinking off the Devon Coast. (Ferry Publications Library)*

The company was able to make this patriotic gesture because of its success in meeting the challenge that the opening of the Suez Canal had presented. The jubilee ships had three-cylinder, triple-expansion steam engines producing 7,000 hp and turning a single propeller giving them a top speed of 16.5 knots. They had a length of 466 feet and a beam of 52 feet. Each ship cost £188,000 and was placed on the company's top links to India and Australia. The first two were built on the River Clyde by Caird & Company whilst the second two were built by Harland & Wolff in Belfast. All could carry 250 first class and 159 second class passengers.

The ships were not fast like their counterparts on the North Atlantic but were broader in the beam and more comfortable in rough seas. The livery that was now adopted by P&O was a black hull, buff deck housing and black masts and funnels. The crews were generally made up of Indians in the engine-room, Lascars (Indian sailors) on deck and stewards from the Portuguese colony of Goa. It has been suggested that the term 'POSH' originated from this time when influential passengers travelling to India had their tickets stamped P.O.S.H, indicating that their cabins were to be located on the portside outwards and the starboard side on the way home, thus benefiting from being on the cooler side of the ship in the afternoon whilst travelling in both directions.

THE CRUISING MARKET

By this time, the nature of P&O's trade had altered radically as revenues from the Royal Mail contracts were diminishing whilst those from passengers and cargo were increasing. In the space of 20 years the size of the fleet had increased from 80,000 tons to 200,000 tons and the run to Bombay had been reduced in time by more than a week. P&O was Britain's premier shipping company serving the Far East and very much an Imperial institution. It still had close ties with the British and Indian Governments allowing its vessels to be chartered for such uses as hospital ships and troop transports when the need was necessary. The company was doing well yet still wanted to explore ways of generating new revenue streams. It was about this time that Arthur Anderson's idea of using P&O vessels for cruising was reconsidered as by this time other shipping companies were beginning to advertise their own particular cruise ship services, in particular, the North of Scotland, Orkney and Shetland Company who began cruising to the Norwegian fjords in 1886 and the Orient Line which started cruising to the Mediterranean and Scandinavia in 1889. Both these companies had found success at an early stage and quickly turned this new industry into a handsome profit for their owners. This did not go unnoticed by P&O who would later acquire both companies. Their success gave P&O the impetus to purchase a 23-year-old ship called the *Rome* and convert her into the company's first ever real cruise ship in 1904. Built by Caird & Company in 1881, the *Rome* was just over 5,000 gross tons and her steam engines could provide around 850 horse power giving her a top speed of around 12 knots. Renamed the *Vectis* she was more of a luxury yacht for the rich and famous than a cruise ship for the masses but she served the company well for eight years before being sold to the French Government in 1912.

One thing P&O had not planned for was the sudden expansion in cheap immigration travel which simply exploded at the start of the 20th century. Much has been written about this phenomena, especially the two most famous companies plying this trade across the North Atlantic, the White Star Company and the Cunard Line. Their ships had grown in size and speed in two completely different ways with one going for speed over comfort and the other going for comfort over speed. This culminated in the ultra-fast *Mauretania*, *Lusitania* and *Aquitania* being built for Cunard and the luxurious *Olympic*, *Titanic* and *Britannic* being built for White Star; but for P&O the story was rather different. Up until 1910 they had concentrated all their efforts on the Royal Mail runs and the passage of wealthy first class passengers which is why there was no third class on their 'Jubilee' class of ships. In 1910, P&O decided to take over the Blue Anchor Line which was a well-known, family-run business sailing between Britain and Australia around South Africa taking emigrants and cargo on the outbound journey and tea and wool on the return journey home.

It had traded well in small, efficient, if sparsely appointed vessels until 1909 when the company was struck by disaster as their newest and largest vessel, the *Waratah* disappeared without trace on a voyage back to the UK with the loss of all 211 people. The company never fully recovered from this disaster and the takeover by P&O in the following year was welcomed by many of the old employees of the Blue Anchor Line who felt that as part of the P&O empire they had a greater chance of holding onto their jobs and a more prosperous future. With the acquisition of the Blue Anchor Line, P&O could now trade at both ends of the passenger market with first class passengers travelling to India and Australia via Suez and third class passengers going via the Cape.

P&O GOES TO WAR

As for Thomas Sutherland, he had now been with P&O for almost 60 years and was very close to retirement. In 1914 two major events took place that were to shape the future of P&O. Firstly P&O merged with the British India Company allowing Sutherland to retire and for the British India's Chairman, Lord Inchcape, to take control and secondly the Great War started with over 100 ships from the P&O group of companies being requisitioned by the Admiralty for military service. Within 24 hours of war being declared P&O's first requisitioning took place when the *Himalaya* was ordered to Hong Kong for fitting out with eight 4.7 inch guns. She became an armed merchant cruiser protecting trade and shipping in the China Sea. In Britain two further P&O ships, *Mantua* and *Macedonia* were also similarly converted and this was all in the first week of the war. Convoys started to leave India to support the British Expeditionary Force in France with over 30,000 Indian troops being moved in one convoy alone.

Considering the amount of tonnage that was lost during the Great War (around 15,000 ships sunk in all) P&O came out of it relatively unscathed. Their worst loss occurred on 30th December 1915 when the 7,974 gross tons *Persia* was torpedoed in the Mediterranean near Crete. Nearly 500 feet long and with a beam of 53 feet, *Persia* was powered by the highly advanced, triple-expansion steam engines capable of driving the ship at over 18 knots. She was attacked by U

boat *U38* at around midday whilst most of the passengers were having lunch, killing 343 of the 519 people on board. The ship had gone down with a huge fortune of gold and gems belonging to the Indian Maharaja Jagatjit Singh who had fortunately not been on the ship at the time of the sinking.

The proudest moment for P&O during the war was when Captain Archibald Smith of the *Otaki* was posthumously awarded the Victoria Cross after his ship engaged the German surface raider *Moewe*. As a civilian, Captain Smith was not entitled to be awarded the Victoria Cross and his exploits were kept secret as it was viewed that military recognition of the defence of his ship would affect treatment of merchant prisoners of war.

The last ship lost by P&O during the conflict was the *Suranda* which was torpedoed on 2nd November, just nine days before the Armistice. In all P&O lost around 500,000 tons of shipping throughout the Great War but due to the increase in shipbuilding capability, managed to finish it with roughly the same amount of tonnage that it had started with.

FLEET EXPANSION

At the end of the war there was a strong rumour that P&O was about to purchase Cunard when in fact they finally bought the Orient Line and the Khedivial Mail Line. This was as in addition to the Union Steamship Company which was bought in the last full year of the war. P&O's requisitions did not stop there with the General Steam Navigation Company being purchased in 1920 and Strick Line in 1923. Of the 300 plus German civilian ships that had been seized by the British Government at the end of the war, P&O bought 98 of them as passenger traffic rose sharply after the end of hostilities.

A company milestone was reached in 1923 when *Mooltan* and *Maloja* became the first ships ordered by P&O to be over 20,000 gross tons. A second company milestone was reached in 1924 when for the first time ever P&O recorded a profit of over £1 million. This allowed the company to go on a major spending spree where the four famous 'C' class ships were introduced. The *Cathay*, *Comorin*, *Chitral* and *Corfu* were all over 15,000 tons and were powered by two four-cylinder quadruple-expansion steam engines, each powering its own propeller and giving a service speed of around 16 knots. They were 547 feet long and over 70 feet wide and could carry 203 first class and 103 second class passengers on the company's premier service to India and Australia. All four ships were built by Barclay Curle & Company on the River Clyde with the first two being launched on the same day by Lord Inchcape's wife and daughter.

It did not stop there with the larger and equally famous 'R' class following on with the *Rajputana*, *Ranchi*, *Ranpura* and *Rawalpindi*. These were improved versions of the 'C' class and could take 307 first class and 288 second class passengers. All the 'R' class were built at the Harland & Wolff shipyard in their lesser known yard at Greenock in Scotland and upon entry into service, were placed on the prestigious run to Bombay.

P&O's most famous ship of this time was the Royal Mail

Narkunda was the **Naldera**'s sister in the Australia service. She continued until 1942 when she was sunk by German bombers, having landed troops at Bougie in Algeria. (Bruce Peter collection)

Steamship *Viceroy of India* which entered service in 1929. Originally ordered in April 1927 under the name *Taj Mahal* she was just under 20,000 tons and built by Alexander Stephen & Sons on the Clyde. She was appropriately launched on 15th September 1928 by Dorothy, Countess of Halifax, the wife of the then Viceroy of India. The 'Viceroy' was revolutionary in that she was only the third vessel in the world at that time to have turbo-electric machinery rather than steam expansion engines for her propulsion. Compared with other passenger ships in the P&O fleet at that time, the *Viceroy of India* was a fast ship, having a service speed of 19 knots which allowed her to break the London to Bombay record with a time of 16 days 1 hour 42 minutes soon after entering service in September 1932. The accommodation aboard *Viceroy of India* was truly astounding for a ship of her size, with much of it being designed by Elsie MacKay, the daughter of the P&O Chairman. She was the first P&O ship to have an indoor swimming pool and the first to have individual cabins for all of her first class passengers. The quality of her appointments was not restricted to the higher grade passengers alone. P&O had designed the interiors of this ground-breaking vessel so that comparable advances were made in the level of comfort enjoyed by all classes throughout the ship. She was the last P&O ship to be built with the traditional black hull and black funnels for Lord Inchcape decided to paint the hulls of his next and final order of ships gleaming white with buff funnels. This was to be applied to all new P&O ships from this moment forward and is a policy that continues to this day.

This last order of Inchcape's was for five ships which were to become known as the White Sisters or the 'Straths' after the lead unit, *Strathnaver*. She was launched on 5th February 1931 at Vickers Armstrong Ltd of Barrow in

Furness by Lady Janet Bailey, second daughter of the P&O Chairman. This new ship was big by P&O's standards but much smaller than the liners on the crack North Atlantic run which by now had reached over 80,000 tons in size. The new ship was 639 feet long and 80 feet wide. She had a total gross tonnage of 22,547 tons and could carry 498 first class passengers and 670 tourist class passengers as second class were now to be known as. She sailed on her maiden voyage from London on 2nd October 1931 to Australia via Marseilles, Suez, Bombay and Colombo. The second ship was *Strathaird* and followed her sister into service a year later in 1932. This was a very sad year for the P&O Group as it lost its charismatic and popular Chairman, when Lord Inchcape suddenly died.

DEPRESSION AND ANOTHER WAR

Lord Inchcape had been rewarded by the British Government for P&O's contribution to the war effort of 1914-1918 and the subsequent drive to get the British economy moving with an Earldom back in 1929.

He remained in charge of P&O until his death by which time the company was starting to feel the effects of the great depression and passenger numbers were dropping. The amount of cargo being carried had been reduced significantly and even the Royal Mail contracts could not generate the huge profits the company had seen during the previous decade.

The Chairmanship of P&O fell to Inchcape's son-in-law, the Right Honorable Lord Craigmyle who guided the company through the financial strains of the 1930s where the company forced its staff to take a ten per cent pay cut and more often than not did not pay out any dividends to its shareholders. Despite this downturn in passenger numbers the company decided to continue with its order for the

White Sisters and in 1935 Vickers Shipyard delivered *Strathmore*, closely followed by *Stratheden*. Both were slightly larger than the first two sisters and were instantly recognisable as they only had one funnel compared to the three of the first two ships. The fifth and final sister was *Strathallan* which entered service in 1938 and was the last P&O ship to enter service before the outbreak of World War II. On delivery of this last ship, Lord Craigmyle retired due to ill health.

At the outbreak of hostilities, the P&O group had a total of 368 ships and just as in the First World War the company was to make a significant contribution to the British war effort. By the end of September 1939, all of the 'R' class were under Royal Navy control including the *Rawalpindi* which was requisitioned by the Admiralty on 26th August 1939 and converted to an armed merchant cruiser by the addition of eight 6 inch guns and two 3 inch guns. She was set to work from October 1939 in the Northern Patrol covering the area around Iceland. While patrolling north of the Faroe Islands on 23rd November 1939, she investigated a possible enemy sighting, only to find that she had encountered two of the most powerful German warships, the battleships *Scharnhorst* and *Gneisenau* which were conducting a sweep between Iceland and the Faroes. The *Rawalpindi* was able to signal the German ships' location back to the Home Fleet in Scapa Flow. Despite being hopelessly outgunned, the ship's 60-year-old Captain, Edward Kennedy (the father of broadcaster and author Ludovic Kennedy), decided to fight, rather than surrender as demanded by the Germans. He was heard to say, "We'll fight them both, they'll sink us, and that will be that." The German warships sank *Rawalpindi* within 14 minutes but not before she managed to score at hit on *Scharnhorst*. A total of 238 men died when the *Rawalpindi* sank, including Captain Kennedy and 54 of the 65 P&O men still on board. Some 37 men were rescued by the German ships and a further 11 were picked up by another P&O ship, HMS *Chitral*. Captain Kennedy was posthumously Mentioned in Dispatches when clearly something like a Distinguished Service Order or even the Victoria Cross would have been more suitable. The Prime Minster, Neville Chamberlain, told the House of Commons, "They had no thought of surrender. They fought their guns until they could be fought no more. Their example will be an inspiration to those who come after them."

The loss of *Rawalpindi* so early in the war was P&O's worst shipping disaster in the whole conflict. Other ships were lost including *Viceroy of India* which was torpedoed on 11th November 1942 off Oran and the *Cathay* just moments later. In one operation to launch a head on the North African coast P&O lost over 110,000 tons of shipping including the almost new *Strathallan*. From the invasions of Italy to D Day and the Normandy Landings, P&O ships were in support of the Royal Navy as either troop carriers, armoured cruise vessels or as hospital ships. They continued to support the British war effort right up to the end of hostilities in 1945 by which time they had lost 182 ships with a combined tonnage of over one million tons and over 1,000 serving crew members.

World War II had taken a great toll on P&O but everyone knew that it could have been much worse.

AIR TRAVEL PROVIDES COMPETITION

P&O's headquarters in Leadenhall Street, London, had miraculously survived the Blitz so on Wednesday 18th December 1946 the company held its first post-war Annual General Meeting. The company was now lead by Sir William Currie and he outlined the future plans by stating that

*Strathaird (illustrated) and her sister **Strathnaver** introduced a distinctive new look to the P&O fleet; they were the epitome of the tropical ocean liner in the 1930s. (Ferry Publications Library)*

*The launching of **Orsova** at Barrow-in-Furness in 1954. The vessel cost £5.7million at the time. (Barrow Museum)*

passenger traffic would be concentrated on the Australia, India and China runs whilst more emphasis would be placed on its cargo business. He acknowledged that air travel would become a major player in the travel industry and that P&O should embrace this new technology and work with it rather than against it. He wanted to build new ships that were cost effective and economical to run. The company ordered its first new passenger ship, *Himalaya* which, at cost of £3 million, was the company's most expensive ship by some distance. *Himalaya* was built by Vickers Armstrong in Barrow in Furness and had a gross tonnage of 27,955. She was also very fast with a top speed of 25 knots which would cut the UK to Bombay passage by five days and reduced the overall voyage to Australia from 38 days to just 28 days. By the time she entered service with P&O in 1949 much of the company's profile had changed and the number of cargo ships outnumbered the passenger ships by three to one.

The decline in passenger numbers meant that as older tonnage was sold off or scrapped, it was not necessarily replaced as the number of passenger ships leaving P&O far exceeded the number being built. Just a total of six new ships were built for P&O from the end of World War II to the start of the 1960s including *Chusan* of 1950 and the second *Arcadia* in 1954. A smaller version of the *Himalaya*, the *Chusan* had a tonnage of approximately 24,215 gross tons and a capacity of just under 1,000 passengers. She was built by Vickers Armstrong in Barrow as a direct replacement for *Viceroy of India* and was approximately 646 feet long and 85 feet wide. She was launched on 28th June 1949 and christened by the wife of Viscount Bruce of Melbourne, entering service on 1st July 1950. The new ship was extremely luxurious and well received by both her passengers and crew. One of the reasons for this was that *Chusan* was the first passenger ship to be fitted with anti-roll stabilisers which brought a new level of comfort to her

passengers that had never been experienced before. No doubt it was a result of *Chusan*'s sea-keeping qualities that she was chosen to go on P&O's first world cruise in April 1954. *Chusan* was also the first P&O ship to visit Japan after the end of World War II when she visited Yokohama in November 1950. She also closed the company's scheduled services to India when in January 1970 she left Southampton for the final time on a direct sailing to Bombay.

The second *Arcadia* was built by John Brown shipyards on the Clyde and was launched on 14th May 1953. She was slightly larger than *Chusan* at 29,734 gross tons and served on the Australia run for her entire career until she was retired in 1970. Both *Chusan* and *Iberia* undertook many cruises from London and Southampton to the Mediterranean and other more exotic destinations such as Asia and South America.

Such was the success of the new jet airliner that passenger numbers continued to dwindle and in the middle of the 1950s P&O were to order the last two ships which were to serve on any of their company's scheduled services. In what was a gloomy period for the company, no one ever envisaged that they would go on to have such long and successful careers and that one of them would become one of Britain's most famous and best loved ships of all time. In 1955 it was announced that two new large and extremely fast passenger ships would be delivered for the Australia service in 1960. The first would go to Orient Lines and would be called *Oriana* whilst the second would be for P&O and in reference to the company's strong ties with Australia, would be called *Canberra*.

NEW SHIPS FOR A NEW AGE

On 3rd November 1959, HRH Princess Alexandra launched *Oriana* at the Vickers Armstrong shipyard at

*Top: **Arcadia** dressed overall during a cruise to Alaska in 1970. (FotoFlite)*

*Above left: **Arcadia**'s First Class lounge, showing the ornate carpet supplied by Templeton's of Glasgow, who commissioned the photograph. (Bruce Peter collection)*

*Above right: The First Class library on **Arcadia**, again showing a carpet by Templeton's. (Bruce Peter collection)*

Barrow in Furness. She was the last ship ever built for the Orient Line as the company was fully absorbed in the P&O operations in 1966 giving the corporation a new name of P&O Orient Lines. As a result, when she entered service she still wore the Orient Line traditional colour scheme of a corn-coloured hull with white superstructure and corn-coloured funnels. Her maiden voyage was from Southampton to Sydney in December 1960 and at 41,915 gross tons and a capacity for 2,000 passengers in two classes (first and tourist), the *Oriana* was briefly the largest passenger liner in service on the UK to Australia and New Zealand route, until the introduction of the *Canberra* in May 1961. The *Canberra* had been launched by Dame Pattie Menzies, wife of the Australian Prime Minister Robert Menzies, at Harland & Wolff on 16th March 1960. She was the last passenger liner ever to be built at the famous Belfast shipyard which could pride itself on the construction of some of the biggest and most famous passenger ships of all time.

The *Canberra* was the most technically advanced ship built by P&O since the *Viceroy of India* back in 1929. All of her engineering spaces, and subsequently her funnels, were placed at the after end allowing vast open areas in the middle of the ship to be developed as passenger areas. She was the first P&O ship to be fitted with bow thrusters to assist manoeuvring and had a real cinema on board as well as full air conditioning throughout. Arguably the single most remarkable feature of *Canberra*'s design was her turbo-electric propulsion system. Instead of being mechanically coupled to her propeller shafts, *Canberra*'s steam turbines drove large electric alternators which provided power to electric motors which, in turn, drove the vessel's twin propellers. They were the most powerful steam turbo-electric units ever installed in a passenger ship with around 42,500 horse power per shaft.

All of today's modern cruise ships are powered in a similar fashion with large diesel engines replacing *Canberra*'s steam turbines. As if this was not enough, *Canberra* also had another feature which made her unique and set the standard for all of today's large cruise ships. Her lifeboats were placed three decks lower than usual for ships of her type and were recessed into the hull to allow improved view from the passenger decks. This was not only much safer for the passengers as in an emergency the boats did not have to be lowered right from the top of the ship but it also allowed for a huge amount of open deck space to be made available to the passengers. This proved an immediate success for her mainly British passengers who have an unrivalled love of being outside when at sea.

Once *Canberra* had entered service some of the older ships in the fleet were retired and P&O settled down with a fleet of just over 20 ships, of which most were of reasonably modern tonnage. By the mid-1960s air transport had killed off all of the trans-Atlantic passenger traffic and was now eating into the Australian routes as well. P&O's profits were hit hard and the new chairman, Donald Forsyth Anderson, had to make some very difficult decisions which involved selling and laying off ships and of course cutting the number of people that they employed on their services. Despite the ongoing problems of the Suez Canal and the occasional

mishap, including *Oriana* colliding with an American aircraft carrier and *Canberra* catching fire, the two ships became firm favourites of the company and were much loved by their loyal passengers.

By the start of the 1970s things were not looking too good for the company and they began to dispose of all their ships which were not making a profit or did not have a future with the company. The *Chusan*, *Orcades* and *Iberia* were all scrapped in the Far East, the *Himalaya*, *Orsova* and *Oronsay* soon followed leaving *Oriana*, *Arcadia* and *Canberra* as the mainstay of P&O. The solution to their long-term futures was to turn these ships into one-class cruise ships and for P&O to concentrate on the holiday market as a way of returning these giants back into profitability. The P&O board saw a great future in this area of leisure, especially in the North American market where cruising was far more popular, no doubt due to the year-round hot weather in the Caribbean and the fact that the average American had more disposable income than his European counterpart. This persuaded the board to buy the successful American company of Princess Cruises in 1974 and from this point onwards the cruising arm of the P&O Group was to be known as P&O Princess Cruises.

With their change to cruising, *Oriana* and *Canberra* settled back into a regular routine, which would see them both based in Southampton and operating two and three-week summer cruises. *Oriana* would spend the winter months based in Sydney with *Arcadia* whilst *Canberra* would start the New Year with a three-month world cruise. In 1977, the Chairman of P&O announced that the passenger division had made a £4.1 million profit in the previous trading year as opposed to a loss of £6.9 million in 1975. In 1979 the decision was taken to scrap *Arcadia* as she was seen as being too old and outdated for any future use with the company, her place in Sydney was taken by *Oriana* leaving *Canberra* as P&O's sole ship sailing out of Southampton.

P&O AND THE FALKLANDS CONFLICT

The conflict began on Friday, 2nd April 1982, when Argentina invaded and occupied the Falkland Islands (and, the following day, South Georgia and the South Sandwich Islands) in an attempt to establish the sovereignty it had claimed over them. On 5th April, the British government dispatched a naval task force to engage the Argentine Navy and Air Force before making an amphibious assault on the islands. The conflict lasted 74 days and ended with the Argentine surrender on 14th June 1982, returning the islands to British control. In total, 649 Argentine military personnel, 255 British military personnel, and three Falkland Islanders died during the hostilities

At the time, *Canberra* was at the end of her world cruise and heading through the Mediterranean back to the UK. Captain Dennis Scott-Masson received a message asking for his estimated time of arrival at Gibraltar, which was something of a surprise to him as it was not on the ship's itinerary. When he called at Gibraltar, he learnt that the Ministry of Defence had requisitioned the *Canberra* so that they could use her as a troop ship and he was to immediately sail to Southampton. Other ships in the P&O

fleet that were requisitioned included the educational cruise ship *Uganda*, the two ferries *Norland* and *Elk*, the tanker *Anco Charger* and a general cargo ship called the *Strathewe*.

In all, 860 crew members would remain on P&O's ships and sail to the South Atlantic with the hastily assembled 'Falklands Task Force'. After returning to Southampton *Canberra* was modified from her cruising role into a ship more suited to her military role and sailed for the South Atlantic on 9th April, four days after the main task force lead by HMS *Hermes* and HMS *Invincible* had left Portsmouth. On board *Canberra* were units of the Parachute Regiment and Royal Marines who were going to take part in the landings to retake the Islands. The Cunard ship *Queen Elizabeth 2* was also requisitioned but it was decided that she was too much of a national icon to be sent into a war zone which meant that *Canberra* was going to have to do most of the dangerous work and be sent right into the heart of the conflict.

Operation Sutton was the codename for the amphibious assault to reclaim the Falkland Islands and as part of that assault *Canberra* anchored close to San Carlos Sound just after midnight on 21st May. She went forward at around 05.20 that morning unloading her troops throughout the day and under constant attack from Argentinian aircraft. The air attacks on the ships in San Carlos Water continued until 16.00, after which time HMS *Ardent* had been sunk and HMS *Argonaut* damaged. At 19.00, the order was given to disembark the remaining troops from *Canberra*, and at 22.42 she weighed anchor and headed out of San Carlos Water and North Falkland Sound. *Canberra* had landed around 2,000 troops and without sustaining any real damage during the day's events. She then sailed back to Ascension Island where she picked up another set of troops from *Queen Elizabeth 2* before sailing back to San Carlos water and again offloading her troops in the thick of the

battle. She then waited off the Islands until she was ordered back into San Carlos Sound for a third time on 15th June, this time to repatriate captured Argentinian solders back to South America.

Following the Argentinian surrender, *Canberra* and *Norland* took around 6,000 prisoners of war back to South America and after 94 days at sea, the Great White Whale, as the military had affectionately named the *Canberra*, returned to Southampton in what was without doubt one of the most spectacular and emotional home comings the city had ever seen. Her Captain was awarded a CBE and made an Aide-de-Camp to Her Majesty the Queen; a very fitting tribute indeed.

After her return to civilian life and a lengthy refit, the *Canberra* returned to cruising with P&O Princess Cruises. Her role in the Falklands War made her very popular with the British public and many of her cruises were sold out months in advance. She was now Britain's most famous cruise ship and P&O started to think that the conditions were right for the company to consider ordering a brand new cruise ship, the first since the *Canberra* herself had entered service back in 1961. Before any new ship could be discussed, P&O celebrated their 150th anniversary with a lavish celebration on 7th July 1987 on board the Princess Cruises ship, *Pacific Princess* which had been moored up in Greenwich, London just for this special occasion. The highlight of the evening was a Gala dinner of which Her Majesty the Queen and the Duke of Edinburgh were the guests of honour.

Once all the euphoria of the 150th celebrations had calmed down, P&O put together a team under the name of Project Gemini to work on the new ship and after much consultation a new 69,000 gross tons cruise ship called *Oriana* was ordered from the German shipyard of Meyer Werft in 1991, after the first *Oriana* had been sold in 1986.

Oriana fitting out at Barrow-in-Furness on 3rd November 1959. (Barrow Museum)

Top: *An impressive view of* **Canberra** *at speed. (Mick Lindsay collection)*

Left: *The panoramic view of* **Canberra***'s First Class Bonito Pool – a feature only made possible thanks to her aft-located machinery. (Bruce Peter collection)*

Above: *Dancing in* **Canberra***'s Tourist Class Island Room. (Bruce Peter collection)*

ENTER THE NEW ORIANA

Delivered in April 1995, the new ship was named by Her Majesty the Queen in Southampton and upon entering service immediately became the largest and most expensive ship that P&O had ever owned. She was an outstanding success as demand outstripped supply with all of her cruises fully booked months in advance. When *Canberra* was compared to the new ship it was clear that she was outdated in so many ways that it would be impossible to bring her up to the same standards. The fact that *Canberra* was a much more fuel-thirsty vessel was the final nail in the coffin and in late 1996 it was announced that the most popular cruise ship the company had ever owned would be withdrawn from service. Her final cruise left Southampton on 10th September 1997 for a 20-night cruise around the Mediterranean, during which she met up with the new *Oriana* in Cannes where passengers were able to go across in tenders for a visit on P&O's latest flagship. Later the same day, the 'Golden Cockerel', a large metal silhouette of a cockerel on a pole traditionally carried by the fastest ship in the fleet, was handed over to *Oriana* in a ceremony eagerly watched by passengers of both ships. Upon her return to Southampton the ship destored before heading to Pakistani ship breakers where it took over a year to dismantle one of the last passenger ships ever built in the UK.

To replace the *Canberra* it was decided to order another brand new ship from Meyer Werft which would be even bigger than the *Oriana* and to transfer *Star Princess* from Princess Cruises to P&O where she would become the third ship to be called *Arcadia*. As the British cruise market continued to grow it was decided to also transfer the *Sea Princess* which would become *Victoria* giving P&O three ships until the arrival of their new vessel after the millennium. The new ship was named *Aurora* on 27th April 2000 by Princess Anne at a lavish ceremony in Southampton before setting off on her maiden voyage on 1st May. Regrettably this was aborted after just a few hours when a stem tube bearing overheated and failed causing the ship to return to Southampton before heading back to Germany for emergency repairs. She finally entered service later that month with a ten-night cruise to the Canary Islands.

P&O PRINCESS CRUISES PLC AND CARNIVAL

Just before *Aurora* entered service it was announced that all cruise ship operations were to be de-merged from the P&O group, forming a new independent company which would be known as P&O Princess Cruises PLC. This new company would also operate the other passenger shipping companies now owned by P&O including the German cruise company Aida Cruises, the river cruise company, A'Rosa Cruises and Ocean Village Cruises, a new company which was aimed at the younger and less formal market. The whole company would become independent of the P&O Group but would remain under the control of P&O's latest Chairman, Lord Sterling of Plaistow.

In April 2003 P&O Princess Cruises PLC was bought out by the American Cruise Company, Carnival Corporation, after an initial offer from rivals Royal Caribbean Cruise Lines was turned down by the P&O Board. This made Carnival the world's biggest cruise operator with more cruise ships than anyone else. Apart from Carnival Cruises itself the company also owned Holland America Line, the Italian cruise company, Costa Cruises as well as Cunard which it has purchased from Trafalgar House in 1998, meaning that the two giants of British shipping were now owned and operated by the same American company.

As soon as Carnival had completed the purchase of P&O Princess Cruises it split the company into its own individual brands which would all be controlled by the parent company from the US. This meant that P&O would now be branded as P&O Cruises with its own head office in the UK and its own set of directors which would steer the company into the 21st century.

The success of *Oriana* and *Aurora* was assured with

*The very popular **Sea Princess** was built in 1965 by the John Brown & Company shipbuilders on the Clyde as the **Kungsholm** for the Swedish America Line. She entered service for P&O Cruises in 1978 and served with both P&O and Princess Cruises before having her name changed to the **Victoria** in 1995 to allow the present **Sea Princess** to acquire the name. (Bruce Peter collection)*

*The beautiful lines of the new **Aurora** are immediately recognisable in this photo of her leaving the German shipyard of Meyer Werft for the North Sea in February 2000. (Meyer Werft)*

record numbers of people now sailing from the UK on P&O Cruises ships. The demand was increasing at such a significant rate that Carnival took the bold decision to transfer two of Princess Cruises' new 'Sun' class ships to P&O Cruises which at around 77,000 tonnes were similar in size and capacity to *Aurora*. Known as 'The White Sister', *Ocean Princess* and *Sea Princess* became *Oceana* and the *Adonia* and the two vessels were renamed together in Southampton on 21st May 2003 by HRH The Princess Royal and her daughter Zara Phillips, the first double ship-

naming ceremony in history.

Carnival's plans for the expansion of P&O Cruises did not stop there with an announcement that they were to get a brand new ship which for the third time in less than ten years would be the biggest ship the company had ever owned. One of the advantages of belonging to Carnival was that it brought with it a wealth of talent in cruise ship design and operation such as with the Holland America Line who since their acquisition by Carnival had three new ships built which were collectively known as the 'Vista' class. The

*The unmistakable sight of St Mark's Square in Venice is the backdrop as **Arcadia** slowly glides into the World Heritage port. (P&O Cruises)*

Azura was the second P&O Cruises ship to break the magic 100,000 ton barrier. Like her sister, **Ventura**, *she is a magnificent ship that offers a wonderful range of amenities for just about everybody. (P&O Cruises)*

'Vista' class was a Panamax (Panama Canal maximum size) design of ship with a tonnage of around 85,000 tonnes and room for just over 2,000 passengers on a hull design that had a smooth and modern appearance. As the third ship in the P&O Cruise fleet to be called *Arcadia* had been transferred to Ocean Village cruising, it was decided that the new ship would become the fourth *Arcadia*. She was launched on 26th June 2004 and entered service with the company the following April. Upon the entry into service of *Arcadia*, *Adonia* was transferred back to Princess Cruises and reverted back to her original name whilst a smaller Princess Cruises ship, *Royal Princess*, was transferred to P&O Cruises and renamed *Artemis*.

The success of P&O Cruises continued to grow as passenger numbers sailing out of Southampton continued to grow at a substantial rate. In the last year of the 20th century fewer than 300,000 people were cruising from the Port of Southampton but, by the end of *Arcadia's* first year in service this number had more than doubled to over 700,000 and the number was still rising. Carnival saw the potential growth and decided that as Britain's most popular cruise line, P&O Cruises were in a good position to take advantage of this expansion so in 2006 they announced that the company was to receive the next ship of their 'Grand' class design which up until now had been exclusively for Princess Cruises, meaning that for the first time ever, P&O Cruise would have a ship of over the magic 100,000 tonnes mark.

THE 'GRAND' VENTURA AND AZURA

The 'Grand' class started life in 1997 when *Grand Princess* entered service and briefly became the world's biggest ever cruise ship. *Ventura*, as the new ship was to be known, was the tenth ship of this design and again was modified from her sisters to suit the requirements of both P&O Cruises and the British cruise market. The keel was laid on 26th August 2006 and launched less than a year later. She was named by Dame Helen Mirren on 16th April 2008 before departing on her maiden voyage to the Mediterranean two days later. Even before *Ventura* had entered service it was confirmed by P&O Cruises that the final unit of the 'Grand' class of ships was going to be assigned to them and that for the second time in two years P&O Cruises would be receiving another ship of over 100,000 tonnes. To be built at the same Italian shipyard of Monfalcone as her sister, the keel of *Azura* was laid down on 27th October 2008 and launched on 26th June 2009 before being handed over to P&O Cruises on 1st April 2010. She was named in Southampton on 10th April by her Godmother, Darcey Bussell, a former principal dancer of the Royal Ballet.

A GRAND EVENT CELEBRATES 175 YEARS

On Tuesday 3rd July 2012, P&O Cruises celebrated their 175th anniversary on what was the wettest July day in living memory. The celebrations, which were over two years

*The dancer and Godmother to **Azura**, Darcey Bussell, poses with the seven Captains of the P&O Cruises fleet to commemorate the 175th anniversary of the founding of the company on 3rd July 2012. (Mike O. Dwyer)*

in the planning, started at around 04.00 when the first of the company's seven ships started to arrive in their home port. *Ventura* was on the Mayflower berth with *Arcadia* and *Aurora* immediately in front of her. The *Oriana* was on the City Terminal with *Azura* on the Ocean Terminal. This left the recently introduced *Adonia* and *Oceana* to fight for the last of the space on the old QE2 berth at dock head. Never before had seven cruise ships birthed together in any British port with a combined tonnage of 569,000 gross tonnes. A logistical nightmare then took place as over 30,000 passengers disembarked or embarked bringing an estimated £17 million to the economy of Southampton.

The dancer, and newest judge of the popular BBC programme 'Strictly Come Dancing', Darcey Bussell, who named the *Azura* back in April 2010, met the seven Captains of the seven ships on the stern of the P&O flagship before unveiling a special plaque to commemorate the occasion in Carnival House.

Later, Her Royal Highness, the Princess Royal, was the guest of honour at a special reception on board the *Oriana* where senior P&O Cruises executives such as the then Managing Director, Carol Marlow and David Dingle, the CEO of Carnival UK at the time were joined by a list of celebrities who have an involvement with P&O Cruises such as Marco Pierre White, Atul Kochhar and Olly Smith. Also present was the life president of P&O Cruises, Lord Sterling. They all enjoyed a sumptuous luncheon which included a special cake baked by celebrity patissier Eric Lanlard.

The weather did not let up and regrettably, the evening

display by the Red Arrows aeronautical display team had to be cancelled. At 17.15 *Adonia*, under command of the P&O Cruises Commodore, Steve Burgoine, slipped her moorings and headed to the top of Southampton water where she turned and slowly started her journey out into the Solent. As she passed each of the other P&O Cruises ships they in turn left their berths and started the procession down towards the open sea. As each passed dock head, a short firework display took place as they slowly lined up for a fleet review. After *Adonia* came *Ventura* followed by the *Arcadia, Aurora, Oriana, Azura* and *Oceana*.

Once in formation the ships were due to be reviewed by The Princess Royal who would be waiting for them off the Isle of Wight aboard the Trinity House Vessel *Patricia*, with Lord Sterling, Carol Marlow and David Dingle also on board. Close by was the Royal Navy's newest ship, the Type 45 destroyer, *HMS Dragon*. To the starboard side of the ship passed *Adonia, Arcadia, Oriana* and *Oceana* whilst to the port side passed *Ventura, Aurora* and *Azura*. Once past the *Patricia* the ships all went their separate ways on their Grand Event Cruises to the Mediterranean, the Baltic, the Norwegian Fjords and the Canary Islands.

ENTER BRITANNIA AND A VISIT FROM HER MAJESTY THE QUEEN

Whilst the company was busy celebrating its proud heritage, plans had been announced that the third of a series of ships being developed by Carnival Corporation, known as the Royal Class, was going to be assigned to the P&O Cruises brand. The first two units of the class were assigned to the Princess Cruises brand and named *Royal Princess* and *Regal Princess* respectively. As P&O Cruises wanted the ship to represent everything that is excellent about being British, it was decided to give the ship a name that was synonymous with Britain's seafaring traditions, yet reflected P&O Cruises representations of contemporary Britain. She was to be named *Britannia*. At over 144, 000 gross tonnes she was to be the largest ship ever built exclusively for the British cruise market and offer a range of new and exciting options such as a cookery school, an enhanced range of premium dining restaurants influenced by P&O Cruises new brand of 'Food Heroes' and for the first time ever on a British ship, all the ship's outside cabins would have their own private balcony, including those for single travellers. The ship would be a modern classic and a statement of P&O Cruises commitment to the future, offering the very best of British cruising with even more new and innovative ideas to help people enjoy their time on board.

The keel for the new ship was laid down on 15th May 2013 and she was floated up during Valentine's Day the following year. She was handed over to P&O Cruises on the 27th February 2015 before arriving in Southampton two weeks later to a rapturous welcome by thousands of well-wishers who had lined the shores of her home port to see her arrive in glorious sunshine. Over the next few days she was shown off to invited guests and the travel trade before a gala dinner for distinguished guests was held on board ahead of her official naming ceremony by Her Majesty the Queen.

Britannia is as contemporary as she is large with a number of firsts for both P&O Cruises and the British cruise market. She is truly worthy of being called P&O Cruises flagship and a fantastic testament to the foresight of Brodie McGhie Willcox and Arthur Anderson. Not even they could have imagined that from their humble beginnings in a small London office, such a huge and impressive cruise ship with the Union Flag proudly emblazoned across her bows would one day carry the name of a P&O Cruises flagship.

P&O Cruises has come of age with its current fleet of diverse and wonderful ships, each with its own unique style and ambience designed to offer something for everyone in their quest for the perfect holiday. Over one million people a year cruise with them on a range of holidays from a two-night party cruise to a world circumnavigation lasting three months. With the introduction of *Britannia*, it is clear that today's management have the same drive and dedication as their predecessors by investing and diversifying in an attempt to meet the challenges of running a successful cruise company in the 21st century. They are without a doubt Britain's favourite cruise company, respected and admired throughout the world for their heritage and a quality of service that is simply second to none. Long may they continue to be so!

Aurora was the first ship in the P&O Cruises fleet to be rebranded in the company's new and vibrant colour scheme. She is seen leaving the city of Hamburg at the end of her 2014 refit. (Blohm & Voss)

Chapter Two

The Birth of a British Icon

When *Britannia* sailed into Southampton Water for the first time on that bright sunny morning in the spring of 2015, it heralded a new era in cruising as P&O Cruises were introducing for the fifth time in 20 years the largest and most innovative cruise ship exclusively built for the UK market. Weighing in at over 144,000 gross tonnes, the company's new flagship blended a contemporary style and image with an impressive technological standard. She was the third unit of the successful Royal Class provided by Princess Cruises' *Royal Princess* and *Regal Princess* but completely reconfigured to P&O Cruises specific requirements. Some 20 years after P&O Cruises took delivery of their *Oriana,* regarded as the first modern cruise liner to have been constructed for the British market, *Britannia* signalled a new stage in the development of the fleet. With its distinct identity reinforced by an adornment of the hull with the Union flag and royal blue funnels instead of the more traditional buff yellow, it was intended to reinforce the pivotal objective of creating a vessel of quintessentially British character in terms of onboard ambience, facilities and service. Registered in her home port of Southampton, *Britannia* is a testament to the dynamism and vision of Carnival UK and a tribute to P&O Cruises and her interior designers.

The story of *Britannia* dates back to February 2010 when the *Azura* was about to enter service and Carnival Corporation's naval architects were putting the finishing touches to a new class of vessel that was to replace the successful Grand Class of ships which had first entered service with Princess Cruises back in 1997. What was needed now was a new breed of ship that was going to be as ground-breaking as the Grand Class, but enhanced with new innovations that would appeal to the more diverse range of people that were cruising in the second decade of the 21st century. Discussions were being held in Miami and Southampton as to how this new design of ship would evolve and what part it would play in the next stage of P&O Cruises progression. The world recession was having a great effect on all aspects of global commerce and P&O Cruises were working very hard to make sure that their product was correctly promoted so they would survive this journey through troubled waters relatively unscathed. The UK cruise market was still showing increases on the number of people choosing to take their holiday at sea but the numbers were not as strong as they were a year or two before. Europe's major shipyards had reduced their costs in response to the global slowdown and for the first time in a decade, were advertising building slots for deliveries in less than three years. Now was a good time for Carnival Corporation to look at their portfolio of cruise lines and decide where to place orders for those brands that showed the potential to increase their capacity.

A BRITISH SHIP WITH ITALIAN PEDIGREE

Princess Cruises were one of the first brands to be selected for a new ship order, along with Costa Cruises and Carnival Cruises themselves. They were to receive the first two of this new class of ship to be named the Royal Class, as it is common practice in the maritime industry for the lead ship of any new prototype to be identified with the class of ship that it represents. The new class would be significantly larger than any other ship in the Princess Cruises fleet, with an enhanced range of facilities and improved technical performance over previous vessels.

*P&O Cruises then Managing Director, Carol Marlow, celebrates the cutting of the first steel plate for the new **Britannia** on 15th September 2012. (P&O Cruises)*

*Top: Flags proudly fly as the stage is set for the keel laying of the **Britannia** at her Italian shipbuilders. (Fincantieri)*

*Above: One of the many steel blocks that will form the **Britannia** waits on the quayside to be lifted onto her superstructure. (Brian D. Smith)*

Right: Transverse and longitudinal stiffeners, known as beams and girders, are attached to the ship's blocks to give her additional strength. (Brian D. Smith)

Each would carry the significant brands associated with Princess Cruises but bring additional choices when it came to dining and recreation.

While based on the same technical platform as that of the Royal Princess, *Britannia* would incorporate some fundamental differences as regards to her interior design, configuration and exterior styling. As with the preceding pair, the P&O Cruises ship would be built by the Italian shipbuilder of Fincantieri at their Monfalcone yard on the Adriatic coast. The Italian giant can trace its roots back 200 years when the company was first recognised as a shipbuilding entity. Over the years it has built around 7,000 vessels and merged with various companies until in December 1959 a wholly new state financial holding

company was formed. Today it is the largest producer of luxury cruise ships anywhere in the world with over 70 cruise ships built in the last 25 years, 61 of them for Carnival Corporation and its subsidiaries. With its three main construction yards at Monfalcone, Venice and Genoa, the company has other yards in Ancona, Naples, La Spezia and Palermo, where repairs and conversions are undertaken along with the construction of other vessels such as mega yachts, naval ships and offshore vessels. With financial backing from the Italian Government, the company has also invested in yards across the world including the Lloyd Werft facility in Germany and several yards in the United States allowing the company to undertake work for the US Navy which otherwise would be precluded. The company also has several subsidiaries which specialise in their own particular field of shipbuilding and repair including the construction of the sophisticated anti-roll stabilisers needed in all new passenger ships.

Today there are three main players in the European cruise ship construction industry. Fincantieri in Italy, STX Europe in France and Meyer Werft in Germany and Finland. In recent times STX has achieved much public recognition with the construction of the world's largest cruise ship while Meyer Werft have always generated large amounts of publicity for their clients with their newbuilds transiting the River Ems from their yard in Papenburg to the North Sea. Fincantieri by comparison have remained almost anonymous but have continued building a large numbers of cruise ships at their various yards to the great satisfaction of their customers. All three companies have invested heavily in cruise ship production and Fincantieri have the capability to complete a large modern cruise ship in less than two years, consolidating their number one ranking amongst the global shipbuilding elite.

The contract to build *Britannia* was signed on 2nd June 2011 and this is known as a letter of intent or a memorandum of understanding between the customer and the shipyard. Once this is signed the shipyard can start to place the many contracts it needs to build the ship with its recognised suppliers and the owner can put together a team to oversee the construction of the ship. As Fincantieri already had an experienced team working on the first two sister ships they were in an enviable position of already having the key personnel in position to start work on the new ship. For P&O Cruises it fell to Carnival UK's Head of Newbuilding, David Pickett, to put together a new team that would work alongside the design and naval architects to finalise the drawings that the ship would be built to. P&O invited many British companies to tender for work on the new vessel and throughout 2011 contracts were signed with over 60 UK-based companies.

SHIPS MODELS AND AERODYNAMIC TESTING

Normally before any construction of a new ship takes place, a model of the ship is made and tested in large experimental water tanks where strong winds and heavy seas are simulated to see how the hull behaves in extreme weather conditions.

Model testing is crucial to decipher the optimum design of a ship's hull which has the minimum resistance for the desired cruising speed. Sea keeping is a compromise between speed and stability and these tests allowed for the best design to be calculated for the required specification. Although hydrodynamics are able to calculate the frictional resistance of a hull through water on today's modern computers, the resistance created by the wave making of the hull can only be confirmed by extensive testing. Once this is complete the model is then subjected to various aerodynamic tests in a wind tunnel where the test on the dispersal of exhaust gauges from the funnel and the effect of air turbulence over the ship are recorded and modifications made if necessary. However, as the new ship was to be a continuance of the Royal Class, all the data

recorded when the models for the initial ships were tested would be used on *Britannia*, except for some additional wind tunnel tests that were needed on the new funnel arrangement. The shape of the funnel used on board passenger ships are formed in characteristic shapes depending on the cruise operator and the series of the ship it is based on. The funnel has to be designed so that exhaust gas from the engines does not come into contact with the open deck, the superstructure or the air intakes while making the most use of the appearance design intended by the ship owner.

For *Britannia* it was decided at an early stage to give the ship two funnels so that it had a more pleasing aesthetic look that would make her distinguishable wherever she sailed. Although evocative of an earlier era of ocean travel, a number of ships built in recent years incorporate the twin-funnel arrangement, notably Holland America Line's Vista-class, Royal Caribbean's Solstice-class and the four current vessels of Disney Cruise Line. Fincantieri made every effort to optimise the shape of the funnel to promote the rise of smoke emissions upwards and out of the ship through a collective arrangement of multiple exhaust pipes whilst keeping the decorative structures around the funnel very similar to the original design.

Once all the plans for the new ship had been completed and approved by P&O Cruises the steel needed to construct the ship was ordered by Fincantieri from various steel works across Europe which is delivered by sea direct to the yard in the form of large steel sheets measuring anything between 5mm and 24mm thick. Each is encrypted with an alphanumeric punched code that determines where and when it will be used during the construction stage. The type of steel used in a cruise ship is extremely tensile giving it the strength and agility to make it highly to unlikely to fail if it comes into contact with a heavy object. To make sure that steel used in the construction process is of a suitable quality, P&O Cruises have representatives, who in conjunction with the ship's classification society monitor Fincantieri's work, to make sure it is up to the required standard to gain a certificate of seaworthiness at the end.

THE FIRST STEEL IS CUT

The first major step in the construction of any new ship is the cutting of the first steel plate which will actually be used in the physical building of the ship's hull. On 15th September 2012, a ceremony was held at the Monfalcone shipyard to commemorate the start of the steel cutting for yard number 6231, as *Britannia* had not yet been formally announced as the name for the new ship. This is the date that is recorded as the official start date for the construction process. Representing P&O Cruises at the ceremony was the company's Managing Director, Carol Marlow who said, "The cutting of the steel marks the moment the ship goes into production so for us it is a very exciting time as we go from the drawing board to reality. Her design will make a stunning statement across the entire ship's interiors.

Through their ideas they will imbue the ship with a cohesive personality which works across all the public areas including the cabins, cafes, bars, restaurants and lounges. Richmond's designs will add an elegant and timeless

Britishness to appeal to everyone who steps on board and will facilitate an excellent evolution of the P&Oness our passengers know and love."

Like all modern passenger ships, *Britannia* was to be built to the modular block construction method. This involves steel being formed into large separately numbered blocks which are then lowered into the building dock and welded together. At the beginning of the process giant electronic magnetic cranes lift the steel sheets into the Preparation Shop where they are cleaned and painted with shop primer which is a sort of undercoat designed to protect the steel throughout the production process. After that it is moved to the Fabrication Shop where it is laid in a shallow pool of water and a computerised plasma cutting machine cuts the steel to a pre-arranged shape. The reason it is cut underwater is because temperatures of up to 25,000 degrees centigrade are generated during the cutting procedure and this way, the heat generated is quickly dissipated avoiding a buckling effect on the edges. Huge pressing machines bend the steel sheets into the required form using nothing more than wooden molds before they are moved to the welding shops for assembly into small panels which are around 50 tonnes in size. These sections are then given extra strength by the addition of transverse and longitudinal stiffeners known as beams and girders which are attached to the ship's frames from which the ribs of the ship's cage are formed. These sections are then welded together to form the large modular building blocks used to build the ship. Once this is complete the whole block is moved to the Paint Shop where a second coat of primer is added before the first of the miles of piping and electrical wiring that the ship is going to need is installed. *Britannia* would be made up of 74 prefabricated blocks, the largest of which would weigh nearly 700 tonnes and be used to house some of the ships engineering spaces. In total there would be 32,000 tonnes of steel used in *Britannia's* construction, which is approximately half of her displacement weight of 68,155 tonnes as a light ship. It is worth mentioning here that the ship's gross tonnage does not bear any relation to the weight of steel in her construction. Gross tonnage is a measure of internal capacity which is measured by taking the total enclosed volume of the ship in cubic feet and dividing this number by 100; thus one gross tonne equals 100 cubic feet. Therefore the *Britannia* has a total capacity of 14,373,000 cubic feet or 143,730 gross tonnes.

THE KEEL IS LAID AND BLESSED

Around six months after the first steel was cut, the official keel-laying ceremony took place on 15th May 2013, which was attended by Carnival UK's Chief Executive Officer, Mr David Dingle, and Fincantieri's Monfalcone Shipyard Manager, Mr Carlo De Marco. The first block was numbered DC13PS and was constructed of six pre-manufactured blocks, weighing in at 408 tons and fitted with 214 tons of pipes, cables, insulation and other equipment. It was blessed by the shipyard priest, Father Gildo, before being lowered into the giant building dock where the ship was to be built. A media release from the shipyard stated that the new ship would incorporate the ultimate in technological standards, and will stand out for its innovative but classic design that will complement the grandeur of its size. Once the ceremony was completed, the invited guests were treated to a lavish lunch provided by Fincantieri as construction continued on the new ship.

One of the first major stages of the construction of any new ship is the installation of the main engines and electric motors which will power the ship. They are some of the largest and most expensive parts of the construction project and need to be installed early on in the building of the new ship, otherwise the yard would have to leave large gaping holes in the steel work and this would delay the construction of the new vessel. *Britannia* is powered by a system known as diesel electric and this is the preferred choice of propulsion for most large new passenger ships. This is where very large diesel engines provide power to the ship's electrical generators which in turn provide energy for all of the ship's electrical needs. About 64 per cent of the energy generated goes to the ship's propulsion and engineering requirements whilst the rest goes to the passenger, or hotel side of the ship. The engines on *Britannia* were made by the Finnish company Wartsila, at their Italian factory in Trieste, who are world leaders in marine propulsion systems. Founded in 1834 in the small Finnish municipality of Tohmajarvi, the company has its headquarters in Helsinki and has grown into a leading global conglomerate in the energy business where it provides engines for one-third of all the world's shipping and has offices and factories in over 70 countries including China and Russia. Wartsila produce a wide range of low and medium speed diesel engines for marine propulsion and engine models are generally identified by the cylinder bore which is measured in centimetres and a V or L configuration to indicate whether the cylinders are formed into a V shape or are all in line. The slow speed engines are normally used in freight ships where one very large engine is used to power a single propeller whilst passenger ships tend to go for multiple medium speed engines working on two or more propellers. The electrical plant is based on two 18,000kVA and two 21,000kVA synchronous generators, driven by 12 and 14-cylinder Wartsila 46F-series medium speed engines, respectively. The technologically advanced engine was chosen because not only is it the most efficient engine in its class with an outstanding power-to-weight ratio but it can also run on either heavy fuel oil (HFO) or marine diesel oil (MDO) when being operated within strict coastal or port emissions areas. This fuel switching can take place smoothly and without power interruption across all engine loads and enables the operator to select the fuel according to price, availability, and the need to meet local emissions regulations. The maximum, aggregate power output is 62,400kW with the diesels running at 600rpm. The main machinery is divided between two separate engine rooms, each housing one 12-cylinder and one 14-cylinder engine

Right: Construction is officially underway as the keel block for **Britannia** *is laid on 15th May 2013 in front of the many distinguished guests from P&O Cruises and Fincantieri. (Fincantieri)*

Top: One of the largest blocks used in the construction of **Britannia** is seen here being lowered into position by the two giant Fincantieri cranes in early August 2013. (Fincantieri)

Above: **Britannia**'s two stabilisers are like small aeroplane wings that extend out from the ship's hull to help reduce roll in heavy seas. (Fincantieri)

Right: On a very wet day in September 2013, the author gets an unparalleled view of **Britannia**, perched high up on one of the giant gantry cranes, almost 70 metres above the dock floor. (Brian D. Smith)

Below: Another block is moved into position ready to be lifted onto **Britannia**'s superstructure. (Brian D. Smith)

plus the alternator. This is because *Britannia* has been developed along the safe return to port system where all of the ship's main services are duplicated into two sections so that if there is a major failure in one system then the other will be able to power the ship back to port in an emergency situation.

ENGINES, PROPELLERS AND STABILISERS

The technical team had also elected to use traditional shaft propellers and rudders and not the Azipod propulsion system. Although Azipods do offer smoother running and greater manoeuvrability, they are very expensive to maintain and only the *Arcadia* in the P&O Cruises fleet utilises them. *Britannia* has two 18MW elastically mounted propulsion motors, designed by the German company of VEM Sachsenwerk at their Dresden factory, to actually turn her propellers. The two propulsion motors turn the six-bladed propellers at a maximum 135rpm, conferring a service speed capability approaching 22 knots. An interesting fact about the propeller shafts on *Britannia* are the fact that they use the environmentally friendly Thordon Bearings' Compac system, which employs seawater as the lubrication medium in place of oil.

The seawater is pumped through a non-metallic propeller shaft bearing and returned to the sea following removal of any abrasives. This eliminates the storage, use and disposal of any unnecessary oil. *Britannia's* two propellers are LIPS 6 bladed FP propellers and are made of a mixture of bronze, nickel and aluminum. Each weighs around 22 tonnes and has 5.7 metre wide blades which turn inwards towards one another reducing the cavitational pulsing on the ship's hull and therefore gives the passengers a smoother ride. To assist with manoeuvrability, *Britannia* has three 2,500kW tunnel thrusters at her bow and three at her stern which work in tandem with the two Wartsila spade rudders which the Captain can control through a solitary lever from the navigational bridge, allowing all three systems to work in one single operation. This very high degree of manoeuvrability is required so as to rotate *Britannia* in restricted harbours and at tight berths with no or minimal recourse to tugs unless circumstances or regulations demand. The combined output of the six thrusters is in excess of the propulsion power of many of Britain's merchant ships.

Whilst the hull of *Britannia* was being built, her team of Bridge Officers were away at Carnival Group's state-of-the-art simulator complex in the Netherlands. Located at Almere, near Amsterdam, the Center for Simulator Maritime Training (C-SMART) is equipped with two full mission bridge simulators, six part-task bridge simulators and the means of simulating fixed propeller and podded propulsion operation. C-SMART is also vested with multiple part-task engine room simulators, two full mission engine control rooms and four machinery outstations so that all those responsible for the safe passage of *Britannia* could be significantly trained in her handling characteristics before they actually took control of the ship.

The steel in the engineering spaces on the lower decks is 10mm thick as it has to support the weight of the engines and generators. (Brian D. Smith)

*An early cut away rendition of **Britannia** gives passengers an idea of some of the facilities that will be available on board. (P&O Cruises)*

A VERY SAFE SHIP IS BUILT

For a ship as large as *Britannia*, a tremendously sophisticated safety protection system is required as she has a capacity to carry over 5,000 people at any one time and could be hundreds of miles from land when an incident occurs. The safety systems for the ship include fire detection systems, sprinkler systems, fixed type carbon dioxide gas firefighting equipment, local water fog system, fire doors and watertight doors. In order to properly manage such a large volume of information at the time of an incident, Carnival Corporation has developed a Safety Management System (SMS) to systematically monitor and operate the safety and firefighting equipment used on board. According to the nature and the location of an accident, the system can present the essential information in a clear and logical order to the Captain and crew with the procedures selected from a large number of predetermined ones to assist them in implementing a suitable response. For

example, when a fire is detected, the system gives the location of the fire with the recommendations to control the relevant ventilation fans, fire dampers and fire doors. It is a highly sophisticated system making *Britannia* one of the safest cruise ships in the world.

As cruise ships have got larger in size, they have become more susceptible to the effects of strong winds and heavy seas as their passenger accommodation can create an air draft of around 60 metres. Despite this large superstructure, the centre of gravity of a modern cruise ship is relatively low making them extremely stable vessels. This is due to the use of lightweight materials in the construction of the upper decks and placing the heaviest components of the ship such as the engines and electric generators below the waterline. When you combine this with the fact that these ships are proportionately wider than ships with deep drafts you can begin to understand why modern cruise ships are very comfortable in most sea states.

To help improve stability and increase passenger comfort, *Britannia* was fitted with a large set of retractable fin stabilisers that extend out from the ship's hull just a few feet under the surface of the water. Looking like small aeroplane wings, they are retracted when not required and sit just in front of the main engineering spaces. Made by Fincantieri's military division, they are computer-controlled electro-hydraulic folding fins, and are tilted automatically as the ship begins to roll. The size of these fins eliminated the need for a second set of stabilisers which would have been more expensive and increased fuel consumption.

MILES OF WELD AND NO RIVETS

Once all of these major engineering projects were underway work could begin on the job of constructing the modular blocks that would make up the main passenger decks. Like the engineering spaces before them, each block would be built in the Fabrication Shop before being painted and lifted into position on the new ship by the yard's two giant overhead cranes, which have a combined lifting capacity of over 700 tonnes. As each section was added to the superstructure, it was guided into position by a series of lasers which make sure that the block is in exactly the right place before it is welded to the ship. Welding steel segments together to form a large ship first began in the 1920s but it wasn't for another 30 years before it finally replaced the rivet as the primary method of ship construction. The hull of a large passenger ship built in the 1930s, such as the much-acclaimed *Normandie*, were held together by millions of rivets. In comparison, the modular blocks of *Britannia* would be held together by over 60 miles of weld. Early concerns that welding would not be strong enough for an ocean-going ship soon dissipated as advanced welding techniques have made the weld seam stronger than the steel it is holding together. The width of each seam depends on the size of the steel it is being attached to but on average

*It's smiles all round as Captain Paul Brown, Micky Arison, Arnold Donald and David Dingle formally announce the name **Britannia** to the world's press at a ceremony in London. (P&O Cruises)*

*A view of **Britannia**'s stern shows some of her engineering spaces and voids exposed before the crew accommodation is lowered into place. (Brian D. Smith)*

the width of a seam on *Britannia* was between 4mm and 10mm wide with the largest seams on the bottom of the ship's hull where most of the weight is supported and the steel is 20mm thick.

THE BRITANNIA'S NAME IS ANNOUNCED

At a media conference on 24th September, then Carnival UK's Chief Executive Officer David Dingle announced to the world that the new ship was to be called *Britannia*. There have been two previous ships named *Britannia* connected to the company. The first entered service in 1835 for the General Steam Navigation Company, which went on to become The Peninsular Steam Navigation Company. The second, which entered service in

The Glass House featuring wines by Olly Smith, Sabbatini's Steakhouse being replaced with the The Limelight Club and the layout of the two spiral staircases in the Atrium being altered to one wider staircase at the forward end of the Atrium. There would be no Sky Walk on *Britannia* meaning that the slightly wider and curvaceous balconies of the cabins immediately below the spots on the Princess ships where the Sky Walk joins the superstructure would not be replicated on *Britannia*. As usual with British cruise ships, there would be a smaller casino than on the American ships which would be attached to Brodie's pub rather occupy about three-quarters of the total space in that location.

By the beginning of 2014, most of the steel work was completed and the hull of *Britannia* began to look like the

*The addition of a Duck Tail on the **Britannia**'s stern makes the ship more stable and allows for an increase in weight during any future conversions. (Fincantieri)*

1887, was one of four ships ordered by the company to mark the Golden Jubilee of both Queen Victoria and P&O itself. Standing alongside him was the Carnival Corporation Chairman, Micky Arison, and Paul Brown who was to be *Britannia*'s first Captain. Speaking to the media, Mr Dingle commented that *Britannia* will be a modern classic, a ship for this and future generations offering authentic travel by sea in an enduringly contemporary setting.

As *Britannia* was going to be an evolvement of the Royal Class, specifically designed for the British market, there were going to be some significant differences between the original ships and the British version. There would be an additional pool on the Sun Deck overlooking the stern and some of the cabins on the forward section of the Lido Deck would be removed and replaced with a fine dining restaurant, a function room and the popular Crow's Nest Bar. As expected, there would be detailed differences in the use of spaces such as the Crooners Bar being replaced with

magnificent ship that she was to become. All that remained was to lift the bridge section into position at the front of the ship then the two distinct funnels that would make *Britannia* so recognisable wherever she goes at the stern. The steel work for these sections was so heavy that both of Fincantieri's two overhead cranes were required to work in tandem to lift the blocks into position. With the capability to lift over 700 tonnes, the cranes are synchronised by computer to make sure that they both lift evenly and at the same rate. Guided by lasers, the steelwork is carefully lowered into position before being checked that it is perfectly balanced in exactly the correct place before being welded onto the superstructure.

Like all P&O Cruises ships, *Britannia* would be painted white but with the new royal blue coloured funnels and the Union flag motif across the upper sections of her bow. Many different types of paints are used in the construction of a cruise ship and this was to be applied by a specialist

This bow shot of **Britannia** depicts the main passenger decks under construction with the accommodation decks being formed above them. The lifting eyes on the ship's bow will be sheared off before the next block is lowered into place. (Brian D. Smith)

39

To left: The ship's huge bulbous bow that will reduce fuel consumption as it cuts through the water is slowly lifted into position. (Fincantieri)

*Top right: The stern cabins are lowered into place giving us the first glimpse of **Britannia**'s distinct outline. (Brian D. Smith)*

Above: Just four months after the keel was laid and the steelwork has reached up to deck 11. The open space at the rear of the ship is where the crew accommodation will be. (Brian D. Smith)

*Right: By the end of 2013 a majority of **Britannia**'s hull was in place and the steel work was beginning to resemble a ship. (Brian D. Smith)*

company called Petrolavori who would not only paint the ship but be responsible for the preparation and application of all of the different surfaces that were to be covered. The white outer coat and Union Flag motif is anticorrosive epoxy paint with a polyurethane enamel which has a durable polyurethane finish designed to provide long-term colour and gloss retention of the superstructure. Over 2,000 litres of paint were used in the motif alone. The immersed hull has epoxy paint with a self-polishing copolymer antifouling ingredient that provides protection from abrasion and corrosion whilst minimising future maintenance costs. The internal areas of the ship, such as the bulkheads and open finishes use a paint with alkyd enamel. The word alkyd actually refers to the synthetic resin used as a binder, making it very resistant to normal wear and tear. Each coat is checked three times to verify the correct dryness, film covering and thickness by the builders, the owners and the paint manufacturers. In total, there are some 350,000 litres of paint on *Britannia* which will require a constant maintenance scheme throughout the life of the ship to keep it looking fresh and clean.

Britannia's bulbous bow is rarely seen, yet is a sophisticated piece of equipment that extends over 10 metres in front of the ship. (Brian D. Smith)

FLOATED UP IN THE TRADITIONAL FASHION

As lovers across the world exchanged gifts on Valentine's Day, P&O Cruises got ready to stage their own celebrations with the launch of *Britannia*. The first ceremony that morning involved the welding of some significant coins to the open deck of *Britannia*, which maritime tradition designates will bring the ship good luck. A 1oz solid silver brilliant uncirculated 2013 coin featuring *Britannia* with her trident and shield was chosen to mark the occasion as 2013 was the year the hull was laid. After the coin ceremony, the focus then moved to the dockside where the ship was blessed by Father Gildo, before a bottle of Italian Prosecco was smashed against the hull by the ship's Madrina.

Italian tradition dictates that a Madrina, or Godmother, officiates at a float-out ceremony and P&O Cruises selected Travel Counsellor's Louise Hunt as the Madrina for *Britannia* after a competition was run throughout the travel trade to find the best person possible to fulfil this role. Amongst a cacophony of noise created by the shipyard horns sounding in celebration, the building dock's giant sluice gates were opened to the sea and millions of litres of water were allowed to pour into the dry dock and start to fill the area where *Britannia* was sitting. This is a far simpler and safer way of launching large ships than the more traditional

Britannia's navigational bridge is "flown" across the shipyard ready to be welded to the superstructure just a few days before she was floated up. (Fincantieri)

*With her second funnel now in place the outline of **Britannia** can be appreciated for the very first time on what was a very wet and cold day in January. (Brian D. Smith)*

*The open spaces of **Britannia**'s atrium are cluttered with materials as the engineers and fitters work hard to complete her luxurious interiors. (Brian D. Smith)*

Top left: The second of **Britannia**'s two funnels is slowly lifted off the dock floor on her way up to the very top of the ship.

Top right: The combined lifting capacity of both Fincantieri's dock cranes was required to lift the funnel over 60 metres into the air.

Above: Once in position, the two cranes take the strain whilst the funnel is welded into position.

Right: To successfully paint the superstructure requires a significant amount of scaffolding to be erected.

Below: Her name is painted in preparation for the floating up ceremony.

(All photos Brian D. Smith)

*In her natural element at last **Britannia** glistens in the early spring sun. (Fincantieri)*

***Britannia**'s port propeller is six bladed and constructed of bronze, nickel and aluminium. At a maximum speed it will rotate at over twice a second. (Brian D. Smith)*

method of pushing the hull into the water down an angled slope. After about six hours, the amount of sea water, in the dock equalled the weight of *Britannia*'s hull and as the equilibrium began to favour the sea water she gently lifted off her construction blocks. Immediately the ship is afloat, engineers go inside the hull to check for leaks and any other defects which could compromise the vessel's safety. Once they confirmed that the hull was sound and there was enough water in the building dock to safely move the ship without damaging her, several tugs were attached and *Britannia* was carefully manoeuvred out of her building dock and round to the fitting-out basin where she would be completed over the next nine months or so. During this formal ceremony, then Carnival UK's Chief Commercial Officer, Gerard Tempest said, "*Britannia* will be a market-leading ship for a market-leading brand when she makes her debut in spring 2015. There will be an unrivalled mixture of contemporary sophistication mixed with those enduring hallmarks of P&O Cruises: high-quality service, cuisine and entertainment delivered with style and glamour."

PASSENGER CABINS AND PUBLIC ROOMS

The outfitting of any new ship involves the installation of an enormous quantity of equipment ranging from the navigational equipment on the bridge to the beds in the

*Water slowly rises up **Britannia**'s hull until the point where her weight is exactly the same as the amount of water she displaces when she will float. (Fincantieri)*

*Louise Hunt is **Britannia**'s Madrina and welds the lucky coins to the ship's superstructure just before she is floated up on 14th February 2014. (P&O Cruises)*

passenger cabins. Before any of this equipment could be fitted to *Britannia*, it was necessary to treat all the metal surfaces with various kinds of enamels and resins which would not only provide a smooth and uniform surface to work on, but provide good sound and heat insulation as well as an excellent undercoat for the final covering. Once this has been completed work could begin on installing the luxurious interiors that had been designed to make *Britannia* a very well-appointed ship indeed. The delivery of all this equipment is meticulously planned well in advance so that each part arrives for installation in the shipyard just at the right time and in the right order. When you consider the equipment in the ship's galleys, cabins, restaurants, engineering spaces and other public areas, then you can begin to imagine what a logistical predicament this can be.

One of the principal jobs during the outfitting is the installation of the passenger cabins which are built by the Italian company Santarossa, who have a large purpose-built factory close to the shipyard. *Britannia* would have a total of 1,837 passenger cabins and nearly 700 crew cabins with each cabin being prefabricated off site then transported to the shipyard by road. All of the facilities that you would expect to find in a cabin such as the bathroom, the lighting, the carpets and the furniture is assembled before the cabin leaves the factory. Each cabin has a pre-designated number and is built in a specific order ready to be installed in the ship at the appropriate time. As each cabin arrives at the shipyard it is taken straight to the ship then craned into

This collection of photos demonstrate the mixture of sophisticated plant and simple brushing required to apply the 350,000 litres of paint used on **Britannia***'s hull. (P&O Cruises)*

The main atrium is seen at an early stage of construction looking towards the stern. The 'Star Burst' will hang from the top of the photograph. (Brian D. Smith)

position through a hole which has been especially left on each cabin deck, before being manoeuvred into its designated position by hand. Shipyard workers then connect the cabins into the ship's essential services such as the electricity and the water supplies. Soft furnishings such as the bedding and cushions are added later.

The passenger cabins with their own private balcony do not have the sliding doors fitted to the cabins as these form part of the ship's superstructure and are added before the cabin arrives. Once all the cabins on a particular deck have been installed, the hole in the superstructure is welded shut and checks are then carried out by the shipyard and the owner to make sure that each cabin conforms to the necessary requirements and specification. As each cabin is passed as completed, it is sealed up so that it cannot be accidentally damaged during the rest of the construction period. All this is installed by the contactors working in harmony with the shipyard to make sure that the construction process is not slowed down by unnecessary delays as the ship has to be finished on time or the owner could impose severe penalty clauses for late delivery of a ship which can run into thousands of pounds per day.

Whilst the cabins are being installed work continues on the rest of the ship including some early testing of the major engineering components such as the engines, electrical generators and heating systems. Some of this work cannot take place until the ship goes on her sea trials towards the end of the year. However, a lot of dry-bed testing can take place and this proves invaluable information before the sea trials start. During the testing phase, other equipment is installed such as the air-conditioning units, the huge washing machines for the laundry rooms, the artwork for the passenger spaces, the lighting and stage equipment for the theatre and so on. On average around 40 tonnes of new equipment is added to the ship every day reaching an impressive 13,000 tonnes once the ship is completed.

*Once on the fitting-out quay work continued on completing **Britannia's** interiors, including the decorative ceiling in the Horizon Restaurant. (Brian D. Smith)*

Britannia is captured on the first day of her official sea trials at the top of the Adriatic Sea. Her swimming pools are still covered to allow the construction workers the protection needed to complete their work. (Fincantieri)

*An outstanding view of **Britannia**'s new Union Flag motif at sea as she is put through her paces by the sea trials team. (Fincantieri)*

*Looking like she is on top of the world, **Britannia** is captured through a "fish eye" lens which has accentuated the curve of the earth and created a very dramatic back drop. (Fincantieri)*

FLOORS AND CEILINGS

A good guide to how a ship is progressing is by the installation of the ceilings and floors. One of the first and most intricate parts of the passenger areas to be installed are the ceilings, which in some rooms can cover the full width of the ship. They often have complicated geometric shapes and contain state-of-the-art light, sound, safety and air-conditioning systems. They have to be very robust and conform to the latest fire regulations yet be flexible so that they can absorb the movement of the ship in heavy seas. The same goes for a lot of the bulkhead fixings which too must be hardwearing and fire resistant yet create a luxurious feel that the passengers will enjoy. In contrast, the installation of the flooring is the first indication that the ship is nearing completion as this will only start once the services, ceilings and walls have all been completed. In total there are over 20 different types of floor finishes on *Britannia*, including superior Italian marble, decorative resins and fine woods, all supplied from reputable sustainable sources. Most of the decorative resins are on the outside decks covering the wet areas, the recreation areas and the area where lots of passengers will enjoy nothing more than the traditional British pastime of sunbathing. These resins not only meet all of the latest safety regulations but are designed to look like the traditional teak deck which is far more expensive and not used very often these days.

During the fit out of *Britannia* it had been decided that the ship should be fitted with an Exhaust Gas Cleaning System, more commonly known as an exhaust "scrubber" system. The scrubber systems are a diverse group of air pollution control devices that can be used to remove some particulates and gases from the ship's exhaust streams. The first Exhaust Gas Cleaning System was designed to remove carbon dioxide from the air of an early submarine but today's pollution control devices use liquid to wash unwanted pollutants from a gas stream. This would mean that some of the water chests on *Britannia* would have to be enlarged to allow enough water to be stored to achieve this.

The only way that this could be accomplished was for the ship to re-enter the building dock and have her hull opened up to allow the chests to be installed. The problem was that the dry dock was fully booked with other newbuilds for Carnival Corporation and there was no room to squeeze *Britannia* alongside them. Time was crucial so it was decided to re-dock *Britannia* in late September, just before the keel was to be laid for the new *Carnival Vista*. Once docked, *Britannia* could have her new sea chests fitted along with additional sea intakes and the preliminary fittings needed for the exhaust cleaning system. The whole project lasted for about three weeks and did not significantly alter either the building programme or the ship's projected entry into service.

SEA TRIALS AND THE ADRIATIC

By December, the outfitting of *Britannia* was almost complete, with most of her fixtures and fittings now in place. The major works now were to commission the engineering side of the ship and for the painters, decorators, carpenters, electricians and other sub-contractors to finish off their work and have it accepted by both the shipyard and the owner. It was now time for *Britannia* to leave her place of birth and go out on her sea trials. Normally a new ship will go out on two sets of sea trials known as the Preliminary

Sailing straight for the camera, **Britannia** *looks magnificent as her bow cuts through the Adriatic Sea in the early winter's sun. (Fincantieri)*

Britannia gets some assistance from the tug **Bremen** as she leaves Monfalcone for the very last time on Friday 27th February 2015. (Brian D. Smith)

Sea Trials and the Acceptance Sea Trials. As *Britannia* had been re-docked to have her scrubbers fitted, it was decided to combine these trials into one set of trials that would be conducted just before Christmas. Before any trials could take place, an incline test was performed on the ship where her metacentric height was measured by moving a known weight across the ship and checking the movement of the hull at a predetermined height. This is how the ship's centre of gravity was confirmed. Then, early on the morning of 7th December, *Britannia* left Monfalcone with around 800 people on board, all with different tasks to perform and records to make. The ship still belonged to Fincantieri and was officially known as yard number 6231. She was manned by Fincantieri Officers including the yard's own Captain, Claudio Bellich, and the yard's Deputy Director, Giorgio Gomiero, who had overall responsibility for the sea trials. P&O Cruises officials were on board, including *Britannia*'s future Captain and a number of her Senior Officers who, in reverence to their Italian counterparts wore civilian clothing. The sea trials lasted for six days and during that time various extreme manoeuvres were carried out including putting the ship hard over at full speed and doing an emergency stop. She was run at 100 per cent power over a measured mile so that her official top speed could be recorded and several emergencies, including a complete power failure, were simulated so that the ship's safety features could be tested. To demonstrate the agility of the ship, *Britannia* performed a 'Williamson's Turn', to determine how well the ship would be able to turn around in the event of an onboard emergency. The 'Zig Zag' test was also conducted to demonstrate the ship's ability to rapidly manoeuvre away from danger ahead, while still maintaining her forward course.

Noise and vibration tests were also performed to ensure that there was proper insulation between all staterooms, corridors and public areas. Towards the end of the trials, *Britannia*'s crew took control of her and actually got to drive the ship for the very first time in the deep waters of the Adriatic Sea, many readings were logged by both P&O Cruises and the ship's classification society. *Britannia*'s sea trials were a complete success as she did everything that she was supposed to do and performed very well in everything that was asked of her. Fincantieri had built a very good ship. Once everyone was satisfied that the ship had been fully tested and everything that could be logged had been written down the ship was taken back to Monfalcone for the final phase of the fitting out before her hand over to P&O Cruises.

Safely back at the shipyard, the final remaining soft furnishings, carpets and fittings were added to the ship as the architects and the owner worked with the yard to accept each section of the ship as it was completed, making sure that everything was to the highest standard before it was signed off as accepted. Only once everything had been confirmed as in good working order would the ship be formally accepted by her owner and arrangements made for the final payment to be made to the shipyard as only once the ship was fully paid for would it be released by Fincantieri and officially become a P&O Cruises ship.

A FINCANTIERI TRADITION

Eventually the day came when *Britannia* was to be handed over to her new owners and say goodbye to her place of birth. On 22nd February 2015, Micky Arison, David Dingle, and David Noyes, the recently appointed Chief Executive Officer for P&O Cruises, and other

*With her gleaming new paintwork glistening in the spring sunshine, **Britannia** begins her 3,500 mile delivery voyage to Southampton. (Brian D. Smith)*

Top: As her crew and shipyard works look over her stern
Britannia *slowly edges her way into the Adriatic Sea. (Brian D.
Smith)*

Below: **Britannia's** *name is positioned lower down on the hull to
allow for the long sweep of the new Union Flag motif. (Brian D.
Smith)*

Right: Once the final payment by Carnival Corporation for
Britannia *was completed, the P&O house flag was proudly raised
over her bow in celebration. (Brian D. Smith)*

*Sailing resplendently into the Solent, **Britannia** approaches her home port for the very first time on 6th March 2015. (P&O Cruises)*

distinguished guests joined the ship for a day of celebration. Fincantieri provided a wonderful lunch to celebrate the impending hand over of their latest ship to its new owners during which time, the Italian and Fincantieri flags which had been flying proudly from the ship's mast would be lowered and the P&O Cruises and the Red Ensign raised in their place. The final payment for the new ship could now be made by the parent company and *Britannia* would officially become a P&O Cruises ship. For a few days more the ship remained at her builders as engineers made the finishing touches before she was finally ready to begin her 3,528-mile journey to Southampton and the spectacular celebrations that were planned to welcome her.

At exactly 16.00 on Friday 27th February, *Britannia* released her mooring lines and in a grand traditional fanfare, which included playing Sarah Brightman singing 'Time to Say Goodbye' she gently slipped away and departed her Italian Shipyard for the very last time. Her journey to Southampton took just over a week and included a stop in Gibraltar to take on additional bunkers. On a very bright and sunny spring morning at the beginning of March, the ship was off the Nab Tower at the entrance to the Solent. After the pilot had been taken aboard she slowly began her journey up Southampton Water towards her home port. As she turned off the Isle of Wight and started the final part of her delivery voyage she was met by three tugs, the *Svitzer Sarah, Svitzer Alma* and *Svitzer Ferriby,* who began the traditional welcome for a new ship when they sprayed their two water cannons over the front and rear of the brand new ship. *Britannia* proudly sailed into Southampton where thousands of people had been eagerly waiting to get their first glimpse of the largest ship ever built to serve the British cruise market. Helicopters carried local news teams as a flotilla of small craft escorted the ship up to Mayflower Park where she pirouetted around in a show of agility before reversing in the Ocean Terminal, which was to be her home for the next two weeks.

HER MAJESTY THE QUEEN NAMES THE BRITANNIA

Over the next ten days, *Britannia* was shown to the travel trade and the British media as everyone was eager to get a first glimpse of P&O Cruises impressive new flagship. During this time she undertook a number of short promotional cruises where travel agents and members of the travel industry could get a firsthand experience of the ship that they would be helping to promote. On the night before her naming ceremony, a gala dinner was held on board the ship, compered by the comedian Rob Brydon, who featured in P&O Cruises latest advertising campaign.

A great many distinguished guests associated with P&O Cruises, as well as those involved in the construction of the ship were treated to a wonderful evening of fine dining and entertainment which culminated in an extravagant firework display in front of Mayflower Park.

Finally the day arrived when *Britannia* was to be officially named by Her Majesty the Queen in the presence

With their waters cannon's providing a very spectacular display, the Svitzer Sarah, Svitzer Alma and Svitzer Ferriby accompany Britannia up Southampton Water to a resounding welcome from the people of her home port. (P&O Cruises)

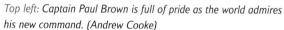

Top left: Captain Paul Brown is full of pride as the world admires his new command. (Andrew Cooke)

*Top right: A flotilla of small craft accompanies the **Britannia** as she nears the end of her seven day delivery voyage from Italy. (P&O Cruises)*

*Above: Through a mist of sea spray the **Britannia** edges closer to the Ocean Terminal and the maiden arrival at her new home. (Andrew Cooke)*

*Right: Members of the Princess of Wales' Royal Regiment, the Tigers Parachute Display Team, present the Union Flag to Captain Paul Brown and the **Britannia**. (Andrew Cooke)*

Britannia is blessed by the Right Reverend Jonathan Frost, the Bishop of Southampton, in front of some very distinguished guests included Her Majesty the Queen, The Duke of Edinburgh, Micky Arison and David Dingle. (P&O Cruises)

P&O CRUISES

*Top left: Captain Paul Brown introduces Her Majesty the Queen to his officers and crew on the bridge of **Britannia**. (P&O Cruises)*

Top right: Her Majesty the Queen and Captain Brown share a quiet word during the official naming ceremony. (P&O Cruises)

*Above left: A very exciting moment as Her Majesty the Queen steps forward to name the **Britannia**. (P&O Cruises)*

*Above right: Her Majesty the Queen is very pleased to meet some of **Britannia**'s crew on her tour of the ship. (P&O Cruises)*

*Right: The moment of impact as the Nebuchadnezzar of the Brut NV smashes against the hull of **Britannia** and the celebrations begin. (P&O Cruises)*

*Her Majesty the Queen, the Duke of Edinburgh and the Senior Officers of **Britannia**. (P&O Cruises)*

of His Royal Highness, the Duke of Edinburgh. On 10th March 2015, the whole world seemed to be watching as Captain Paul Brown invited the Queen to name the ship in a glittering ceremony accompanied by the Royal Marines Band Service, the Band of the Irish Guards, English soprano Laura Wright and a cameo show performed by the BBC's 'Strictly Come Dancing' Team. Upholding its celebration of all things British, P&O Cruises selected sparkling wine from the Wiston Estate Winery in Sussex to name the ship. A Nebuchadnezzar of the Brut NV was used by the Queen while thousands of bottles of Brut NV and Rosé, Vintage 2011 were enjoyed during the various inaugural events that took place around the launch. Everything went off without a hitch and the Royal Party even got time for a tour of the ship before enjoying lunch in one of *Britannia*'s restaurants.

The following day, *Britannia* undertook her last cruise before officially entering service. Known as the cruise to nowhere, it was a short two-day cruise along the English Channel for friends and family of P&O Cruises staff, enabling any last minute teething problems to be sorted out and for the crew to have one last chance to familiarise themselves with the operation of the ship.

Ultimately the time for *Britannia* to start earning her keep and set sail on her 14-night Maiden Voyage to the Mediterranean arrived on Saturday 14th March as 3,600 excited passengers boarded the ship ready to indulge themselves in the wonder of P&O Cruises latest vessel. The band of the Royal Marines played the ship away and as dusk was beginning to fall, *Britannia* cast her morning ropes and sounded her horn. Confetti was blasted over the ship and a glass of champagne handed to every passenger. Streamers were flung from the passenger decks as the customary firework display brightened up what was a cold evening as the port's tugs made sure that the departure was a spectacularly wet occasion. *Britannia* made her way slowly down Southampton Water followed by hundreds of well-wishers in small boats before turning into the Solent and the English Channel. Her life at sea had begun.

Britannia is an embodiment of British culture that encapsulates everything that is good about Britain today. She has won many awards during her first year in service, including the much-acclaimed Best New Ship award for 2015 at the Cruise International Awards. She is a vitrine of British excellence that marries a bespoke style and image with an impressive technological standard. P&O Cruises refer to her as a modern classic, designed for the future with one eye on their illustrious past. To her passengers she is a modern-day marvel, full of innovative ideas that make travelling on her a complete joy. She is the pride of the P&O Cruises fleet and worthy of the title as company flagship. Overall, the ship is elegant and refined and perfectly captures the spirit of modern Britain. It will be quite some time before we see anything like her again.

*Every outside cabin on **Britannia** has its own private balcony with those lucky enough to have a cabin overlooking the ship's stern able to enjoy some memorable sunsets over the ship's wake. (Darren Holdaway)*

BRITANNIA

SOUTHAMPTON

Chapter Three

The Spirit of Britain

Every new day on P&O Cruises stunning new flagship is exciting yet pleasingly different. The beginning of the day is rich with anticipation, the sea stretching into infinity with the sky as the sun glistens on the ship's new paintwork. It is an invitation for you to set your own pace as the ship's attentive crew care for your every desire. For some it is simply settling down on a comfortable sun lounger by the pool and total immersion in their favourite book, whilst for others it is the promise of a visit to an undiscovered destination and the anticipation of what lies ahead. For a few energetic passengers that have been energised by a restful night's sleep, the day could begin with a fitness class or a workout in the gym before breakfast in one of the ship's many restaurants before taking part in a dance or cookery lesson. Then there are the daily lectures in The Studio or the Headliners Theatre featuring big names from the world of celebrity, politics, entertainment and science, all of them guaranteed to have their audiences enraptured as *Britannia* cuts smoothly through the sea on her way to her next port of call.

Morning drifts into midday as the Officer of the Watch tolls the eight bells to indicate that it is now the afternoon and proceeds to explain the ship's performance over the last 24 hours and the prevailing weather conditions. Lunchtime brings forth the second of the day's main dining occasions and the conundrum of either enjoying the waiter service delights in one of the main restaurants or partaking in the choice of delicious tempting treats around the pool such as freshly prepared gourmet hamburgers or a slice of mouth-watering pizza cooked before your very eyes. Most will head to the popular Horizon Restaurant high up on the Lido deck which serves everything from traditional British roasts to healthy Mediterranean cuisine; or possibly one of the huge arrays of fresh salads, cold meats and other delicatessen delights that are on display just asking to be washed down by a glass of Olly Smith's signature house wine or your favourite lager.

By the middle of the afternoon life on board the ship is in full swing as passengers lap-up the best of the sun's rays in between a freshening swim in one of the ship's many pools, as waiters circulate with trays of cold drinks and enticing cocktails to quench your thirst. After all, you are on a well-deserved holiday, passengers are beginning to return from their adventures ashore and one of Britain's most significant contributions to modern life, Afternoon Tea by Eric Lanlard is being served by immaculately dressed waiters with white gloves in the most convivial of locations, the Epicurean Restaurant.

As the sun begins to sink below the horizon, the mood on board *Britannia* changes to one of anticipation. Evenings on board are an event to behold and soon you will see ladies dressed in their finest ball gowns and jewellery accompanied by men of equal distinction as they make their grand entrances down the atrium staircase. Photographers capture the moment as what is an event to be savoured is frozen in time for all eternity. Soon the ship is buzzing as

The name says it all. A place of serene relaxation by the pool. (Brian D. Smith)

A Homage to Blue by Ptolemy Mann graces one of three communicating stairwells. (Mike O. Dwyer)

The brass wall lights in Brodie's Bar are reminiscent of many traditional British pubs across the land. (P&O Cruises)

*Opposite page: One of **Britannia**'s defining features is her atrium and the stunning "Starbust" designed to be the WOW factor that signifies the ship's luxury whilst encapsulating the best of British 21st century design. (P&O Cruises)*

The Blue Bar is the height of contemporary sophistication which you would expect in any world class hotel. (P&O Cruises)

P&O Cruises toured many of London's finest drinking establishments when seeking inspiration for Brodie's Bar. (P&O Cruises)

Over 70 different beers are available in this the most British of institutions. (P&O Cruises)

*With the Blue Bar and Market Café open all day, **Britannia**'s stunning atrium is a wonderful destination in its own right. (P&O Cruises)*

new friends are met, entertainers applauded and an endless variety of culinary masterpieces are savoured. The evening starts with an aperitif in the friendly Crow's Nest bar high above the ship's bows, with floor to ceiling windows through which to catch a last glimpse of the sunset and to chat with recently acquainted friends. Dinner is the culinary delight of life on board wherever you choose to dine, with the gracious Epicurean Restaurant one of the most remarkable establishments at sea. White table linen, beautiful crystal, elegant silverware and dazzling artwork all combine with the very best of fine food and wine to give you the ultimate dining experience.

After dinner, passengers head to the Headliners Theatre where the resident theatre company will perform an eclectic mix of especially produced live productions only available on this ship. Alternatively, there is the chance to take in a tribute band in The Live Lounge or join in with the dancing in The Crystal Room. Some will spend the evening in Brodie's pub testing their wits against fellow passengers in the nightly quiz or demonstrating their singing prowess in front of the karaoke machine to an astounded audience.

Others will enjoy the more sophisticated entertainment offered in The Blue Bar where a live duo accompany the low thrum of discerning conversation that is generated by another day on board the largest passenger ship ever built for the British cruise industry.

The clocks go forward another hour as *Britannia* crosses yet another time zone and passengers start to drift back to

their sumptuous cabins, where the bed will have been turned down and a chocolate placed on the pillow by their cabin steward. Some may take a final stroll on the open deck but eventually everyone will retire into a deep and blissful sleep, ready for another day of anticipation on board *Britannia* where dreams are realised and almost anything can happen.

BRITISH ARCHITECTS NOW LEADING THE WORLD IN INOVATIVE DESIGN

Of course *Britannia* brings her own distinctive style to P&O Cruises celebrated fleet of impressive ships and like all successful creations this is not simply by chance. The ship has been several years in creation by a team of highly dedicated specialists who are all experts in their own particular field of expertise. When P&O Cruises first began discussing what the interiors of their new ship should look like, it was decided at an early stage that the ship should be proudly British. This was nothing new for the company as all of their previous ships had something about them that makes them uniquely British, whether it is the Lord's Tavern on the *Oriana* or the stately Anderson's Bar on the *Aurora*. What all these features have in common is that they are a nod to Britain's proud heritage and not something that celebrates the Britain of today. What P&O Cruises wanted was something that reflected the trend of what being British represented. When the first new ship of the current fleet was introduced back in 1995, Britain was in a very different

Britannia has the largest collection of British artwork afloat and includes work by contemporary vibrant artists such as Claire Burke (top left), Rebecca McLynn (top right), Sarah Medway (middle left), Jessica Mallorie (middle right and Sotis Filippides (bottom right). (P&O Cruises)

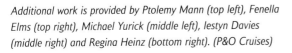

Additional work is provided by Ptolemy Mann (top left), Fenella Elms (top right), Michael Yurick (middle left), Iestyn Davies (middle right) and Regina Heinz (bottom right). (P&O Cruises)

THE SPIRIT OF BRITAIN

*The Crow's Nest bar makes a welcome return to **Britannia** and is one of the few areas on the ship which actually feels like you are at sea. (P&O Cruises)*

Situated next to the Epicurean Restaurant at the vey top of the ship, the Crow's Nest bar helps create an oasis of fine dining that is accentuated with superb views to sea. (P&O Cruises)

place to where she is now. Move forward to today and you will see that there has been a transformation in the way that the world perceives British architecture which has inspired some of the world's most recognisable buildings. London itself is leading the way with many great examples of British construction such as the Shard at London Bridge, the Leadenhall Building in the City and 20 Fenchurch Street with its magnificent Sky Gardens open to the public on the 40th floor. However, it is probably Norman Foster's much-acclaimed St Mary's Axe building which is responsible for this architectural renaissance that has helped London to become an extremely vibrant city and made being British very fashionable again. It was this highly sought after British talent that P&O Cruises wanted to tap into and reflect in their new ship.

As soon as you step aboard *Britannia* you know that you are on something very special indeed. She is a modern classic with an eye for the future. Sophisticated, glamorous and graceful are all superlatives that have been used to describe the ship and it is clear that her builders have drawn upon their vast experience to ensure each element has been delivered to perfection. Colours of red, white and blue combine with superior materials and exceptional furnishings to create a truly contemporary British sensation which is very pleasing to the eye. In fact, when you walk around *Britannia* it is very difficult to imagine that you are on a ship at all, such is the design of her public spaces, but more a world-class luxury hotel that you would expect to see in London's Mayfair. That is because for the first time in the history of P&O Cruises, one company was entrusted to design the ship's interiors and by using just one designer all the interior spaces emanate a cohesive personality which helps create that distinctiveness that you associate with a particular ship. Being given the opportunity to create the space which will enrich the lives of the people who will inhabit it on a complex piece of machinery where your ideas are constrained by the many requirements of maritime law can be very challenging for those who are more accustomed to designing luxury hotels, so it was quite a surprise when P&O Cruises announced that the respected British designers of Richmond International had been selected to design the interiors for their new *Britannia*. Although relatively new to the cruise industry, Richmond International had a wealth of experience in interior design employing around 45 full-time people from the head office next to the Barbican Centre in London.

Founded 50 years ago by Robert Lush and Philip Kitchingman, their list of clients spans 40 countries and includes some of the world's most outstanding hotels such as the Trianon Palace & Spa in Versailles, the Four Seasons Gresham Palace in Budapest and Britain's Langham Hotel in London. A combination of sensitive restoration and complete transformation, employing the skills of many specialists including silversmiths, ceramists and mosaicists, have all helped Richmond International build a pedigree of creating something that is simple yet inspiring. It is for reasons such as this that P&O Cruises went to Richmond and asked them if they would be willing to work with them on their new ship.

A BRITISH DESIGNER FOR A BRITISH SHIP

It all started in 2009 when Richmond were approached by Carnival Corporation asking if they would be interested in designing the spa area on one of their new ships which turned out to be the *Royal Princess* for Princess Cruise lines. It was completely out of the blue but apparently one of Carnival's Senior Executives had stayed at the Four Seasons Hotel near Dogmersfield in Hampshire and had been particularly impressed with the way Richmond had renovated the old 18th-century stable block into a contemporary luxury spa yet had remained sympathetic to the building's original intention. One of Richmond's Directors, Terry McGillicuddy, and other key personnel were invited on board the *Ruby Princess* to see how they could look at ways to bring their ideas and designs to a large floating resort. They quickly identified what worked well and where they could bring their own touch and make some unique improvements. An example of this was the relaxation area being positioned next to the lively gym, so people who were trying to unwind were finding it difficult to immerse themselves in a tranquil environment. Looking at other ships in the fleet it was clear that cruise lines preferred to put the gym and relaxation areas alongside places such as the hair salons and treatment areas so that it could be marketed as the 'Well Being' area. Richmond could see that there would be advantages if this area were to be split up and diversified so they suggested to Princess that the spa area should be moved to another deck on the ship and separated from the gym. Once they explained their rationale behind the decision and the benefits to their passengers, the owners bought into the idea and you now have the Lotus Spa which is available on the *Royal* and *Regal Princesses.*

The senior executives at P&O Cruises liked the way that Richmond had approached the spa on the two Princess ships and that they were not afraid to try something completely innovative. They took a big interest in the company and spent some time visiting their eclectic mix of modern and traditional hotels to get a feel for what Richmond International could do for them on a bigger scale. It was in 2011 that Richmond's Directors were invited to Carnival House to be asked if they would consider designing the interiors for P&O Cruises as yet unnamed new ship. Their brief was to come up with something that was contemporarily British and have some sophisticated wows. The ship was to be a modern classic that captured some of the heritage of the British Isles. The interiors were to resemble an outstanding luxury hotel that would appeal to people who liked to stay in hotels when they travelled. The new ship should reflect Britishness in every way that was possible yet be fit to be called P&O Cruises new flagship. P&O Cruises wanted a new design that would not alienate existing customers but would also attract a new breed of customers who are from an increasingly wide and diverse background to cruising. Of course Richmond sought inspiration from P&O's nautical history as this was a new experience for them that no one had ever taken on before but they relished the opportunity to try something

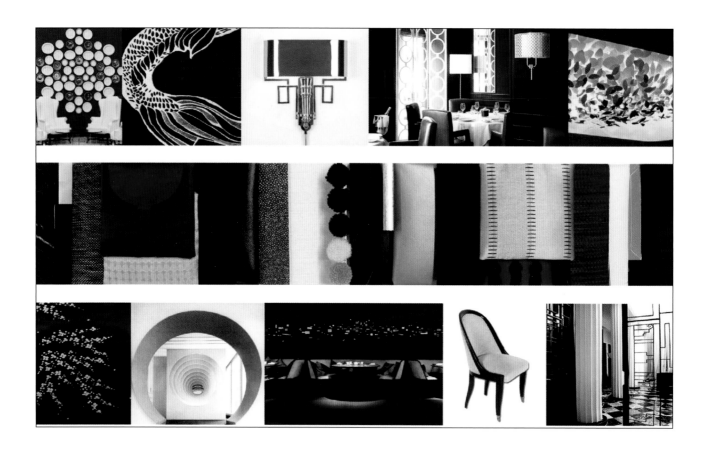

Page 76: One of Richmond International's mood boards demonstrates the colours, textures and finishes being suggested for the Epicurean Restaurant at an early stage of the design process. (Richmond International)

Page 77: An alternative mood board for the Epicurean Restaurant shows photographs of a similar restaurant that was designed by Richmond International to give a flavour of what is to come. (Richmond International)

Page 78 Top/below: Here we see the mood boards for the Oriental Restaurant (top) and the Horizon Self Service Restaurant (below). (Richmond International).

Above: The final mood board is for the Sindhu's Restaurant where the chef's Indian Heritage is reflected in the textures and finishes. (Richmond International)

new and to be associated with such a high-profile project.

No matter how good a ship looks on paper, it is her completed interiors that dictate whether or not she will be accepted by her passengers and deemed a success by her owners. In today's modern world of cruising, passengers have a lot more choice with a vast number of cruise lines and an abundance of cruise ships to choose from when deciding where to take their next holiday.

Some will have particular favourites that they enjoy travelling on whilst others are more flexible in their decision making and will not be influenced by a cruise line and its branding of its ships. Whereas in the last century each cruise ship was an individual with vast differences between sister ships of the same company, most of today's newbuilds are identical in every detail apart from a change of colour scheme and choice of finishes. Of course this is all down to the cruise line's desire to offer a constant product of recognisably high standard across all of its fleet so that every passenger can know what to expect when they travel on one of its ships. To that end, modern ship designers can be constrained when it comes to designing the interiors as any thoughts they might have of developing a new and individualist approach to a project must be balanced by the owners' desire to use its branding throughout the ship as well as the need to increasingly think about revenue potential. Despite all this, most of today's new cruise ships have a very impressive and luxurious feel to them which makes them destinations in their own right. The list of amenities available to passengers means that there is normally far more for them to do on board a ship than any destination that they might be sailing to. As a British company with almost all of its passengers coming from the UK, P&O Cruises are very mindful that any of its new ships must have an appeal that will resonate with its mainly British clientele. A hard task indeed but that is why on any of their ships you will not find a swathe of strong dominant colours or brash materials because these things are not appreciated by the British traveller. What you will find are quintessentially British touches such as the traditional pub, smaller dining areas, cabins with baths and lots of quiet places to rest, all designed with soft unobtrusive colours and subtle finishings to create the perfect environment that could be described as British elegance.

The Crystal Room is **Britannia**'s Show Lounge where the palette of subtle gold and pale blue is complemented by elegant floral decoration, which is carried through the room and onto the balustrades. (P&O Cruises)

Sumptuous surroundings enhance the dining experience and make the Epicurean Restaurant the ultimate restaurant at sea. (P&O Cruises)

Individual private alcoves make you feel like you are in your own exclusive restaurant. (P&O Cruises)

*Olly Smith's Glass House on the **Azura** was regularly voted as the best bar at sea. His establishment on **Britannia** is proving to be equally as popular. (P&O Cruises)*

A CONTEMPORARY DESIGN FULL OF BRITISH MAGNIFICENCE

So where do you start with a project as large and as complex as *Britannia*? For Richmond International it started with the atrium and the heart of the ship. Once they had signed the contract to design the interiors for *Britannia*, they travelled on several other cruise ships to see how things worked well and what they could do to bring their own personal touch to *Britannia*. Apart from the spa area already mentioned, they quickly identified the ship's main atrium should be the social heart of life on board and a destination in its own right. With such a large space they decided the atrium needed to be alive for most of the day and had to have one of the ships 'wows' that would generate its own personality. That much sought after identity for *Britannia* generated a plethora of ideas and suggestions from ornate statues to water features and remarkable light fittings that would hang from the ceiling through the various decks, each designed to give the ship a feel that would help create the right atmosphere on board. After much deliberation and discussion it was one of Richmond's own designers who hit upon the famous 'Star Burst' and what was to become one of the biggest wows ever created on a modern-day cruise liner. The 'Star Burst' is an eight metre high, illuminated centrepiece which hangs high above the atrium floor, suspended through three decks to the seating area below. Visually it is captivating and grabs your attention as you enter the room. Its vastness takes your breath away drawing you in so that you can see that it is actually made up of hundreds of metal and acrylic parts that are illuminated in different ways to help match the mood of the ship. It is a remarkable piece of engineering, taking its inspiration from the stars used as historical naval references and a tangible link with P&O Cruises maritime history. Created by Jona Hoad, the frame for the 'Star Burst' is of a triangular design engineered by engineers Packman Lucas, specifically for its rigidness and strength that has the ability to flex with any movement of the ship. The design allows for most of the metalwork to be attached at the top of the frame with shards of acrylic gradually becoming more prominent towards the tip of the base. As the small pieces of metalwork are so intricate, Jona Hoad used trombone manufacturers in Sheffield to finely polish the tiny fragments of metalwork before attaching them to the main frame. The lighting for the 'Star Burst' is computer controlled and was designed by Maurice Brill Lighting to reflect the ambience in the atrium. It can either be discreet with low level lighting that is appropriate for after dinner drinks or brightly dazzling with a party atmosphere suitable for a gala celebration. To show P&O Cruises how they envisaged the 'Star Burst' would appear on the ship, Richmond hired out a large photographic studio and hung their preliminary ideas from the ceiling.

Only once this full scale mock-up was completed could

*The self service restaurant on **Britannia** has been designed with inspiration from the sea and has blue as its predominant colour. (P&O Cruises)*

The self service stations in the Horizon Restaurant are spacious and have been designed to optimise the flow of passengers at busy times with larger display counters and an improved selection of food available. (P&O Cruises)

The artwork in the Horizon Restaurant includes bronze synchronised swimming figurines that are harmonious with the designer's nautical theme. (Mike O. Dwyer)

Eric Lanlard's cakes are a temptation beyond belief and can be found in the Market Café on Deck 5. (P&O Cruises)

everyone actually see what the designer was trying to create and how it would look on the ship. For the first time it was obvious that this imaginative piece of artwork was really going to set the paradigm by which *Britannia* was going to be judged and that this truly imaginative piece of engineering would be a proclamation of *Britannia*'s grandness.

At the forward end of the atrium is an attractive hand-decorated curved staircase linking all of the atrium's three levels. Finished in the same bronze as the rest of the atrium's railings, it contains a number of lights secreted in the uprights to subtly illuminate the stairs, and more importantly, the people on it as they transcend to engage in their social occasion. When Richmond submitted their initial ideas to the shipbuilders for consideration they did not envisage the curved staircase actually inside the main square but set it back towards the front of the ship. However, the shipyard pointed out that there was a riser in that piece of space so it could not be used to house the staircase. The only option was to move it into the atrium itself. It was one of the many challenges Richmond's had over design. As with all professionals, everything was worked out to perfection and it was this respectful relationship with Fincantieri that went a long way to achieving Richmond's designs for the new ship.

The colour scheme for *Britannia* is mainly light pastel colours with punches of nautical blue and swathes of dark grey palette. This is extensively used throughout most of the public spaces on the ship, whilst the use of tasteful materials effuses a synergy that reflects the ambitions of the architects and the ship's owners to create an exclusive but enjoyable atmosphere. The carpet around the atrium was provided by Brintons who have been manufacturing carpet in Kidderminster since 1783 and have provided carpets for all of the current P&O Cruises fleet. It resembles a traditional British maze which isworked around the square centrepiece that has blue coloured seating for 12 people. On the lower floor around this are a number of chairs and tables which are upholstered in a leather cream or blue fabric. A combination of the two colours decorate the various scatter cushions and soft furnishings that adorn the chairs and tables with unobtrusive mood lighting that can be adjusted according to the time of day. In keeping with Richmond's desire to have this area open most of the day you have the new Market Café on the Portside, which serves cakes by one of P&O Cruises 'Food Heroes', Eric Lanlard. Mustard-coloured bench and table seating is interwoven with biscuit-coloured marble, decorative metal panelling and large brightly lit display cabinets, which with an abundance of natural light create an enjoyable location to drink a coffee with friends or relax after returning from a busy day ashore. An interesting feature of the café is an extremely large word puzzle with the name of the Market Café in embossed font that was designed by the architects and the graphic designers Jackson Daly, who have worked with Richmond on many of their ambitious projects, to

The Market Café is the ideal place in the heart of the atrium for tempting savoury dishes, ice cream in "grown up flavours" and of course, cakes and pastries made by master patissier Eric Lanlard. (P&O Cruises)

The warm colours of the Java Café combine with the excellent sea views to create the perfect place for a relaxing coffee. (P&O Cruises)

The Live Lounge is a high-energy pluralistic room with a large stage for live entertainment that also doubles up as the ship's night club. (P&O Cruises)

*Unlike the previous two units of the Royal Class, **Britannia**'s live venue has a bar incorporated into its design. (P&O Cruises)*

The Marlow Room is a multi function room which can be used for games tournaments, conferences, lectures or even weddings at sea. (P&O Cruises)

*Like **Azura** and **Ventura**, **Britannia** has three main restaurants for her passengers to enjoy the fine cuisine that P&O Cruises are rightly famous for. (P&O Cruises)*

make sure that all the signage was necessary and part of the artistic design. It was Jackson Daly who came up with the ingenious tube-style maps of *Britannia* for the wall-mounted location plans that you will find in the ship's stairwells and other public locations.

Across the atrium is the Blue Bar which P&O Cruises wanted to be a strong visual statement. As a result the counter is decked out in rich black marble with crystal glass with the soft furniture having a plush blue and silver theme. Artistic bar stools complement cylinder-shaped chairs whilst comfy seating is arranged around metallic black tables with illuminated glass surfaces that would not look out of place in an exclusive club or five star hotel. The rear wall has a mysterious dusky look to it that has been illuminated by objects that resemble the planets of the solar system whilst an intricate curved glass chandelier manufactured by Kalmar Lighting to reflect the shape of the Blue bar covers the length of the serving area.

Artwork by Brooklyn-based artist, Randall Stoltzfus, and the Dorset-based glass sculptor, Amanda Notarianni, can be enjoyed in a quiet alcove that is partitioned from the bustle of the main atrium where silk curtains hanging from the windows create a more distinct place to relax and enjoy a drink. By combining a café and a bar across the entire width of the atrium floor with plenty of open seating, P&O Cruises have created a vibrant social hub and achieved Richmond's desire to have the heart of the ship alive and welcoming all day long.

Adjacent to the atrium on Deck 5 on the Portside is the ship's Reception Desk and Explorers, where passengers can interrogate the many new interactive pods that display the range of shore excursions on offer. Black and coffee-coloured marble floors work with polished mahogany veneers and simplistic artwork to create an area that is business like and functional yet warm and inviting before moving up to the second level of the atrium and the many retail outlets that *Britannia* has to offer. Unlike other P&O Cruises ships, these are all on one level and purposefully grouped together on the Port and Starboard sides to offer a substantial amount of space in an open plan environment that has been inspired by some of London's most fashionable department stores. A large amount of popular and luxury goods are displayed in carefully selected panelling and beautifully crafted display cabinets, which are designed to give the area a softer feel without impeding the flow of passengers using the atrium to move around the ship.

On the upper deck of the atrium is the Java café which mirrors the style and sophistication of a London coffee shop. This most harmonious of rooms is a mixture of brightly coloured furniture arranged between a covered promenade giving wonderful views out to sea at the top of the atrium where you can sit and watch the world go by. The colour scheme is predominantly red and can be described

Fine artwork from a significant number of British artists is displayed throughout the ship and is designed to capture the spirt of modern Britain. (P&O Cruises)

as bright and vibrant with a relaxed feel about it. Large wooden display cabinets and a zig-zag patterned carpet contrast with the black hand-laid marbled floor and counter to give a cosmopolitan feel to this very popular area which is infused with natural sunlight making it the perfect location at all times of the day for a light bite with your favourite cup of coffee.

Opposite the Java café is The Glass House which one of a number of alternative dining venues that can be found on board *Britannia*. Here you can enjoy a specifically chosen menu that is designed to accompany the fascinating range of wines that have been chosen by Olly Smith, specifically for *Britannia*. Richmond spoke with Olly and asked him what he liked about his Glass House on the *Azura*, which was his first establishment with P&O Cruises, and what he thought would work well on *Britannia*. He told them that he liked everything about it. To that end, Richmond's knew that for The Glass House to be a success on the new ship they would have to take some of the influences from *Azura* and use their own ideas to create a new and delightful bar and restaurant. The finished product has a very spacious and airy feel about it with several wine towers that rise from the floor to the ceiling. Naturally there is a lot of glass and a large bar in the round is the centrepiece with a mixture of greens and dark wood working well with discreet lighting to create a very stylish restaurant that is a sophisticated space of traditional glamour with a modern twist. Just like the Java café opposite, there are extremely large windows where passengers can sit and eat whilst enjoying the superb views out to sea. In the Glass House, Olly Smith has selected a brand new range of around 40 wines to enjoy by the glass including new labels from Japan, Greece and Croatia. There is also a new menu of small plates such as sea bass ceviche with lime, main courses such as a Wagu beef burger, Morecombe Bay & Devon crab sliders and lobster buns as well as a selection of great British pies and sharing puddings for everyone to enjoy.

WELCOME TO P&O CRUISES 'FOOD HEROES'

Food plays a big part in *Britannia* experience so Richmond took the opportunity to discuss their ideas for some of the other ship's restaurants with the P&O Cruises 'Food Heroes' that would be working on the ship including Atul Kochhar, James Martin and Marco Pierre White. Before designing Atul Kochhar's Sindhu restaurant on *Britannia*, Richmond took senior P&O Cruises Executives for dinner at Atul's Benares restaurant in London to get a taste for the flair and creativity that would be conveyed on their new ship. Situated on Deck 7, the Sindhu restaurant is a conception of rich and deep base colours where the art and lighting play a huge part in the overall ambience. All of the works from the different sculptures are in varying textures that reflect the chef's Indian heritage and help create an aura of intimacy by the use of artistic room dividers that are beautifully crafted to blend in with the Kashmirian art by

Atul Kochhar's Indian restaurant with a twist is spacious yet comfortable with its colour palette inspired by nature and oriental spices. (P&O Cruises)

From the ship's self service restaurant, to the main dining rooms, the division of space has been carefully considered to create a more intimate feel. (P&O Cruises)

The Peninsular Restaurant has a more traditional layout with larger tables and glass pillars. The colour scheme is a musky orange with contrasting browns and is open for breakfast, lunch, afternoon tea and freedom dining every day of your cruise. (P&O Cruises)

Halima Cassell and the very large Indian sculptures by Luke Dickinson to really set the atmosphere for the restaurant. Combine this with Atul Kochhar's wondrous modern Indian dishes and you have a very special dining experience indeed. A richly coloured jagged carpet pattern contrasts well with soft white tablecloths and luxurious satin wood finishes to enhance your eating pleasure and make you feel part of an opulent experience, whether you are eating at one of the many tables for two or the Chef's Table in its own private recess where passengers can arrange exclusive dinner parties.

An innovation aboard *Britannia* is the concept of the Limelight Club on Deck 5 where passengers can enjoy a three course meal from a very exclusive menu whilst watching first-class entertainment. Inspired by some of the world's most famous jazz clubs, the Limelight Club is a live music venue where the mood changes every night with the likes of Kiki Dee, Jaki Graham and Madeline Bell performing whilst you dine. Once the entertainment finishes the venue transforms itself into a late night venue where you can dance the night away until the early hours. The club has a wooden dance floor which runs from a raised stage area where you can find an oversized performer's seat and a grand piano right up to the bar by the club entrance. Effective use of frosted glass and amber lighting with burr walnut furnishings and deeply padded seating helps to recreate the atmosphere that is reminiscent of Ronnie

Scott's famous club in London, whilst clever arrangement of the tables and chairs means that everyone gets an uninterrupted view of the entertainment whilst they eat.

Of course these alternative restaurants are just part of the culinary experience that *Britannia* has to offer. As well as the three main restaurants where passengers can enjoy magnificent meals, including gala menus designed by Marco Pierre White, there is the beautiful cream-toned Art Deco inspired Epicurean Restaurant which has been designed to give you simply the very best of British cuisine. Like the rest of the ship it has been fitted out with elegant furniture and luxurious materials where Italian winged back white leather chairs are arranged around tables with white satin table cloths and fine crystal glassware by Ravenscroft. The walls are ordained with gold leave patterns and circular wine towers that discreetly act as room dividers to create a very intimate feel. Alcoves of bench seating for two provide those lucky enough to sit there a very secluded place to dine that creates the impression of your own private restaurant. A sumptuous light blue carpet with streaks of azure combine with abstract seascapes by Michele Griffiths all of which is beautifully lit by ribbons of gold leaf lighting, especially designed by Chelsom Lighting to create a restaurant that offers an extraordinary fine dining experience in a sophisticated yet captivating setting. If anticipation is a sensory delight then waiting to dine in the Epicurean Restaurant is going to be a reward in itself.

The Sindhu Restaurant's Bar on Deck 7 is a refreshing blend of understated sophistication and cool Britannia, making it a great place for a drink. (P&O Cruises)

The Java Café is situated at the top of the main atrium and is just the place to meet for a coffee before going ashore to explore new and exciting destinations. (P&O Cruises)

Making a welcoming return next to the Epicurean Restaurant is the classic Crow's Nest bar, encompassing the very front of the ship high up on Deck 16. It is the definitive room with a view through large windows giving a sweeping panoramic spectacle of the world on three sides, nearly 50 metres above the sea. The room's nautical atmosphere is further highlighted with a collection of maritime memorabilia combining with lots of brass and dark cherry coloured woods making this the only place on the whole ship that actually feel like you are at sea.

The main bar is situated on a raised platform with tall bar stools and high back furniture which enhance the well-groomed aura that this room pervades. As the floor drops down by the windows the furniture is lower in design so that nothing detracts from the fabulous views that its location affords. A grand piano and inlaid wooden dance floor provide additional entertainment should anyone need it, but with a cocktail list with over 100 drinks on it this really is the perfect location to spend some time with family and friends and reflect on just how good life can be.

Next to this oasis of fine dining is the Marlow Room, affectionately named after one of P&O Cruises former Managing Directors, Carol Marlow. It is a multi-function room lavishly decked out in white furniture with a scattering of brightly decorated yellow scatter cushions and wine-coloured table tops where Bridge tournaments and other popular card games can be played. To allow for the room to be used as a conference venue there is a large interactive television screen recessed into the wall so that it is not too intrusive when not being used. Large floor to ceiling windows are dressed by heavy draperies with light netting behind a surrounding of polish walnut veneer that transcends the bulkheads towards the Crow's Nest Bar where frosted glass allow additional light to enter over the bow, yet still give the room its sensation of intimacy.

When anyone boards a cruise ship for the first time, one of the areas they will probably head for is the self-service restaurant, which in the case of *Britannia,* is situated on the Lido Deck towards the rear of the ship. Decorated with nautical blues and lightly polished woods, the Horizon Restaurant is extremely airy with large floor to ceiling windows running down both sides of the restaurant giving unparalleled views out to sea. Four central buffet serving counters span across the middle of the restaurant each serving the same fare. By allowing people to enter from both ends a total of eight entrances to the food areas really speeds up the serving process and allows for a good number of people to select their food and move on in a short space of time. New features include a live cooking station where you can order freshly cooked pancakes, omelette and waffles and a self-service counter located at the adjacent Terrace Bar which is ideal for those wanting to grab a quick bite without having to go into the main buffet area. Clever design of the food display areas and regulation health guards means that P&O Cruises have been able to enhance the food on offer to their passengers and offer a better selection throughout the day. This extremely large room has been broken up with small booths for families and high tables with bar stools to create more intimate spaces to eat in. A variety of different furniture designs combine with

The Limelight Club is reminiscent of some of the world's most famous jazz clubs and offers a quality restaurant where you can enjoy outstanding live entertainment. (P&O Cruises)

The giant word puzzle outside the Market Café covers the entire wall and contains several references to P&O Cruises. (P&O Cruises)

partitions and focal details to create a more intimate feel that is a genuine pleasure to dine in. Large communal hand-washing facilities are situated at all the entrances to the restaurant which means that you are no longer required to be gelled every time you enter.

PUBS, CLUBS AND TIME FOR 'STRICTLY COME DANCING'

As well as the ship's various restaurants there are also many other venues where people can enjoy the hospitality that P&O Cruises are so famous for. Being British, *Britannia* just had to have a classic pub and in fact Carnival UK's Chief Executive Officer, David Dingle, insisted that any finalised plan of *Britannia* must include a traditional British pub. Brodie's bar is named after one of the Peninsular and Oriental's founder members, Brodie Wilcox, and features over 70 different brands of British beer, surely a record for any licensed establishment. P&O Cruises spent months scouring the UK to source a wide selection of beers both from smaller, local, artisan brewers such as such as Chocolate Tom from Robinson's Brewery in Cheshire and Ginger Hare from Bath Ales in Somerset, as well as renowned breweries including Marston's, Greene King's and Fuller's of London. Large circular chandeliers reminiscent of 19th-century drinking establishments that appear to be candle lit are a prominent feature of the pub as are the wooden finishes to the dividers and uprisers. Plenty of wooden tables and richly coloured banquettes all combine to create the perfect atmosphere that you would expect to find in a typical British pub, which is no surprise as Richmond took P&O Cruises Executives on a tour of some

of London's more established public houses to get a feel for what they would like to see on *Britannia*.

The ship's casino is situated on the starboard side of the bar and features a small selection of roulette wheels, poker tables and other assorted gambling machines.

Situated above Brodie's on Deck 7 is a glamorous location with a classic twist known as the Crystal Room. The Crystal Room boasts a palette of subtle metallic tones where azure and white are the predominant colours. There is an illusion of the room being larger than it actually is by the architects coffering the ceiling, mirroring the elements, and focusing the light to emphasise the expanse of the elegant room. Lightly coloured marble with raised seating around an impressively sized wooden dance floor complements the coloured banquettes and soft leather chairs to give the place an artist vibrancy that is really exciting. The immutable attributes of Art Deco where classic elements combine with modernity is the design touchstone of the Crystal Room and this is best represented by the magnificent chandeliers that are a resemblance to the original foyer lighting of London's celebrated Apollo Victoria Theatre. They coalesce with the grand white piano to form an inspired performance area, suitable to host the 'Strictly Come Dancing' themed cruises that *Britannia* has to offer.

At the rear of Deck 7 is the Live Lounge, which as its name suggests, is a high-energy pluralistic room with a large stage for live entertainment that also doubles up as the ship's night club thanks to a very sophisticated sound and light system. A blend of artefacts and artwork all dedicated to the entertainment industry set the tone of the room

Cold

Topside

Shin

Sirloin

Topside

Rump

Thin
Flank

Flank

grated
parmesan

1,5kg chuck beef or
braising steak, cut
into 5cm/2in pieces

Season
to taste

allots

290ml
fresh beef stock

METHOD:

Heat oven to 150C. Make a cartouche:
tear off a square of foil slightly larger
than the casserole, arrange it in the pan
so it covers the top of the stew and
trim away any excess foil.

Then cook for 3 hrs.

The
Cooker
Club

' Mash

THE ONION SOUP

700g onions

50g butter

1.2L
fresh beef stock

garlic cloves

The Cookery Club was developed in association with the celebrity chef James Martin. One of the only cookery schools at sea, this extremely well equipped venue offers passengers the opportunity to experience a range of cooking classes, hosted dinners, demonstrations and tastings. (P&O Cruises)

Top left: Eric Lanlard is rightly proud of his association with the Market Café. (P&O Cruises)

Top right: James Martin is seen in the Spanish Boqueria Market whilst looking for something special for his Cookery Club during a stop over in Barcelona. (P&O Cruises)

*Above: One of the many delights on board **Britannia** are the wonderful afternoon teas created by Eric Lanlard for the Epicurean Restaurant. (P&O Cruises)*

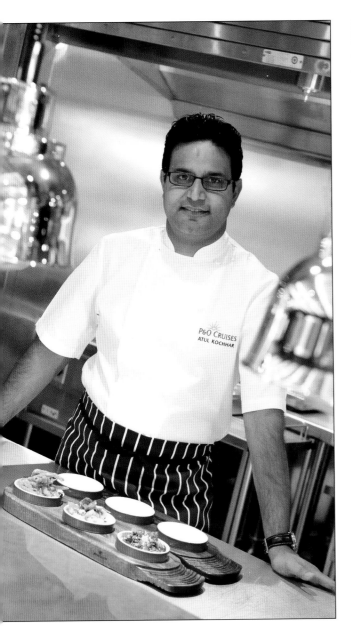

Above right: Another celebrity chef who offers some of his tempting creations to P&O Cruises passengers is Marco Pierre White. (P&O Cruises)

Above left: Atul Kochhar is seen in the kitchen of his restaurant onboard the **Azura**. (Steve Dunlop)

Right: Olly Smith selects wine for establishments on P&O Cruises ships. (P&O Cruises)

Does it get any better? A cookery class taught by Eric Lanlard in one of the finest kitchen establishments created at sea, with panoramic views out across the world. And there is no washing up to do. (P&O Cruises)

The Retreat showcases an oasis of sumptuous calm where you can relax in perfect surroundings and really get away from it all. (P&O Cruises)

With your own private luxurious sunbed, freshly laundered towels, chilled refreshments and your own attentive stewards to look after your every desire, the Retreat represents everything a holiday should be. (P&O Cruises)

Britannia possesses four separate designated age group areas for the children on board and includes state of the art video games, character play times and social hangouts for the teenagers. (P&O Cruises)

where everything from the colours to the textiles are high energy. The focal point of the room is a large central chandelier made up of individually sculptured pieces of metal, illuminated remotely by down lighting that reflect the angular shapes of the room's wall panelling. A funky arrangement of mirrors and glass combining with an eclectic mixture of lighting that is reminiscent of the main atrium but very much jazzed up all work very well together to provide a venue that is ultra-modern and exciting. It is the perfect place to enjoy a range of vocalists, bands, comedians and tribute acts that perform here throughout the day and night.

At the opposite end of the deck is the Headliners Theatre, which is P&O Cruises most technically advanced and features a state-of-the-art LED scenery wall. Situated over two decks it is a substantial sized venue holding 936 passengers and is designed to achieve an effective use of lighting and acoustics at the same time as providing the largest amount of unobscured sightlines to as many people as possible. Seating is of a low back design on one level which gently slopes up over two decks and is fitted out with shorter rows of seats so that people do not have a difficult journey when trying to select their places. The theatre itself is very simple with no decadent artwork or obtrusive lighting to distract you from the stage area. Again more contemporary than most theatres at sea there is no attempt to replicate the traditional theatres of London's West End

but instead you find a more modern and pleasing arena with comfortable seating in blue and grey upholstery, plenty of space to move around in and a private cup holder on the right-hand side of your seat with a shield to protect it from being knocked over accidentally. Discreet lighting is recessed into the mahogany walls whilst lowered handrails around the entrances and passageways mean that no one has an obstructed view. Where the theatre does break new boundaries is its use of a giant light emitting diode (LED) screen across the width of the stage as well as the more traditional fly scenery. The original LED wall concept was overseen by Carnival UK's Entertainments Services Manager, Mr Phillip Yeomans, and was engineered and produced by the Italian company HMS Vadalio. The LEDs are 6mm in length and are formed into 500mm blocks which contain around 2,000 LEDs that can be interlocked to form one giant screen. This allows a lot more creativity in creating the background to the shows that are being staged and allows the set to be changed in the blink of an eye.

A REVITALISED SPA AND A CONCEPT OF INNOVATION

For the first time on a P&O Cruises ship, the Oasis Spa complex is not situated alongside the gym but closer to the reception area in a quieter part of the ship on Deck 5. Once the decision had been made to split the gym from the relaxation area it was decided that the spa would be better

*Situated between the two funnels is **Britannia**'s Sports Arena where a multitude of competitive games can be played. (P&O Cruises)*

The Serenity Pool & Bar, a dedicated space for peace and quiet where you can cool off with a swim before ordering your favourite drink and relaxing. (P&O Cruises)

The Oasis Spa's discreet lighting is key to enhancing the freshness of the space and creating a relaxing atmosphere to complement the dark textural elements. (P&O Cruises)

situated lower down in the passenger areas where it would be quieter and because the great deal of weight associated with the water in the thermal pools would now be positioned closer to the ship's centre of gravity and thus make her more stable. Set in a space of serene beauty, *Britannia*'s well-being area is quite simply the next generation of spa which is the most opulent in the P&O Cruises fleet. With rich warm finishes and swathes of sumptuous dark colours, the reception area features artwork by Fenella Elms and frosted glass that allows natural light to penetrate and infuse with the erotic aromas emulating from the treatment rooms. The spa combines the principles of serenity and movement to create a sanctuary for both the body and mind whilst the decor emphasises relaxation surrounded by luxurious textiles, black marble and polished metals that invite you to experience a sensory journey, providing a tranquil escape with superb views out to sea. Here *Britannia*'s passengers can be rejuvenated in the hydrotherapy suite with heated loungers, heated waterbeds and a saline caldarium where warm saline vapours are used to ease conditions such as asthma and allergies whilst boosting your skin complexion. There is also a hydrotherapy pool with reflexology, massaging jets and air recliners to regenerate the body and allow passengers to relax completely as they get away from it all. The innovative design means that the atmosphere evolves cleverly from one space to the next, so each room creates a different mood depending on your desires. As part of the Oasis Spa,

there is a private villa available for renting by couples or groups named the Oasis Villa. This exclusive space is where you can enjoy your own whirlpool and personal spa therapist for a variety of treatments and massages. There is also a Spa Shop which is a first on a P&O Cruises ship selling luxury skincare and haircare products from deluxe cosmetics brands such as Elemis and La Therapie which are actually used by the beauticians on board.

The gym on *Britannia* has also been moved away from its more traditional space at the front of the ship to a new location alongside the Cookery Club towards the rear of the Sun Deck between the two funnels. It has a light and spacious setting with an impressive range of up-to-the-minute equipment provided by Techno Gym that includes treadmills, bicycles, cross-trainers, free weights and a decent sized wooden aerobics area that is sectioned off from the rest of the gym with a large glass wall. Personal trainers are on hand most of the day to offer advice and support with a range of personal fitness programmes to suit just about everyone's taste and ability.

On the opposite side of the Sun Deck are *Britannia*'s impressive children's areas, an evolvement from the successful children's clubs on the *Azura* and *Ventura* which are so popular with younger families. Designed to offer every conceivable amenity to P&O Cruises younger guests, they allow their parents to enjoy their time on board knowing that their children are in the best capable hands with plenty for them to do. The Reef programme divides the

Effervescent and energising, the Hydropool can be enjoyed by itself or as the perfect prelude to any treatment. (P&O Cruises)

111

*Stylish shopping that is reminiscent of some of the West End's most famous establishments is a feature of **Britannia**. (P&O Cruises)*

A crucial challenge of cruise ship design is making careful use of limited space available. This was particularly pertinent in the design of the ship's cabins which Richmond has cleverly organised to ensure maximum comfort for every passenger. (P&O Cruises)

From the comfortable inside cabins to the spacious suites that have been designed to offer you every possible amenity, you will find each grade of accommodation warmly inviting and boasting ample storage space. (P&O Cruises)

under 18s into separate groups so that activities can be more easily managed and suited to their particular needs with age-appropriate equipment and activities. Named Splashers for the 2 to 4 year olds, Surfers for the 5 to 8 year olds, Scubas for the 9 to 12 year olds and H2O for the teenagers, they each have their own dedicated room with an assortment of toys, games, Play-stations and other pursuits aimed to make a stay on board the ships as enjoyable as possible. All the children's rooms feature soft, brightly coloured anti-slip materials and include climbing frames and ball pools as well as a dance floor that lights up when you dance on it and an outside area where children can play under close supervision from the Reef Rangers.

As well as the Limelight Club, P&O Cruises have introduced two further innovations aboard *Britannia* designed to offer something completely different for the more adventurous passenger. The first is the Cookery Club that was devised and developed by P&O Cruises Food and Beverage team and is situated at the very top of the ship on Deck 16. Everyone at P&O knows how important food is to its passengers and what an essential part of the cruise experience the dining experience can be. It had been a long held an ambition of the company to deliver hands-on cookery classes at sea as they have run cooking demonstrations by their many own talented chefs for many years. These had always been really well attended so it was known that the appetite was there and with *Britannia* they have finally got the opportunity to make it a reality. Run in

consultation with James Martin and featuring the other P&O Cruises 'Food Heroes', such as Marco Pierre White; Eric Lanlard and Atul Kochhar, the Cookery Club can only be described as a world-class cookery school at sea. Designed to offer the most comprehensive schedule of classes for all ages and abilities, the Cookery Club has 12 work stations where 24 people can use an extensive range of cooking utensils and kitchenware in a state-of-the-art facility that simply cannot be bettered anywhere else. With white granite work stations decked out with marble rolling pins, cutting boards and a bank of sharp knives, many of the classes reflect the ports of call where *Britannia* will be visiting. Passengers can go to local markets and vineyards and see speciality producers in the morning before an afternoon class where they will learn how to use the ingredients they have chosen to create unique dishes that they can recreate at home. Large television screens purposefully displayed around the kitchen make sure that everyone gets a close-up view of what the chef is preparing whilst a huge glass wall running the full length of the room gives the very best views to the ocean that cannot be experienced anywhere on land. A private dining area attached to the kitchen allows the students to enjoy the meals that they have prepared in specially arranged gala nights in the company of the celebrity chef and their families.

The second conception is The Studio, which like the name suggests is reminiscent of a television studio with

*Every outside cabin on **Britannia** has its own private balcony, a first for P&O Cruises. (P&O Cruises)*

audience participation. Situated alongside the Photo Gallery on Deck 7, it is a brand new, state-of-the-art, multi-purpose venue which hosts a wide range of entertainment and enrichment options for passengers including the latest films and musical recitals, as well as lectures, guest speakers, cookery demonstrations and of course a wide range of detailed and informative port talks for passengers to make the most of their time ashore.

BEAUTIFUL CABINS AND LUXURIOUS SUITES TASTEFULLY DECORATED WITH YOU IN MIND

Like all P&O Cruises ships, *Britannia* offers a range of accommodation from the ample to the opulent, all of which are a touchstone of harmonious design. Spanning from Decks 8 to 14, there are 1,837 cabins, including the world's first single cabins with a balcony, giving *Britannia* a capacity of 3,647 passengers at double occupancy. All the outside cabins have their own balcony whilst the inside cabins have been carefully conceptualised to maximise the amount of space available and appear very light and airy. Having a yacht-like appearance, the cabins and suites are themed in soft greens or calming blues with three different scenes of

lighting, reflecting some nautical traditions but allowing for a more personal setting when desired. The flat screen televisions have the latest interactive technology that allows you to book shore excursions or make reservations at one of the ship's restaurants whilst balconied cabins have the large floor to ceiling windows that open out onto your own private veranda and allow copious amounts of natural light to penetrate the cabin. All the bathrooms have their own shower screens and decent sized washing facilities that offer a more comfortable experience than on most ships. Superior Deluxe cabins have amenities such as a full size bath, two flat screen television sets and a separate living area with a large comfy sofa and coffee table. These cabins are extremely popular and with a welcoming bottle of champagne and a box of chocolates waiting for you on arrival, they are designed to give you a sense of luxury that you would normally associate with a suite, but at a more affordable price. For some, a cabin is just a place to sleep and change but for others, it is a place to enjoy the ultimate in gracious living whilst relaxing at sea.

Britannia has a range of suites that are situated close to the top of the ship and overlooking the bow and stern. As well as the oversized double bed in its own private

With the company name proudly displayed alongside the new funnel livery, *Britannia* is a showcase for the fresh new appearance of the P&O Cruises fleet. (Brian D. Smith)

The traditional ship's library is a compact affair which reflects the modern preference for many people to use their own Kindles and other electronic devices whilst at sea. (P&O Cruises)

The Studio is another first for British cruising with a fully equipped television studio that doubles as a cinema and a venue for guest speakers. (P&O Cruises)

bedroom, there is a whirlpool bath, a changing area, a large balcony with superior furniture, two flat screen televisions with DVD player and stereo, and a dining area where you can enjoy an elite menu served to you by your own private butler. Luxuriously finished in porcelain and polished granite, the bathrooms have twin basins, separate shower unit, heated towel rails and a range of personal toiletries from the White Company. Those lucky enough to be spending their holiday in one of these magnificent suites will also be able to enjoy their breakfast in the Epicurean Restaurant which is set aside exclusively for suite passengers every morning.

As cruise ships have got larger in size, their owners have had to become very creative to accommodate the large number of people wishing to spend their time in the open air, especially on the warmer sea days which can put a lot of pressure on what is a premium commodity. Richmond have been very creative at the top of *Britannia* in offering a wide range of outdoor amenities that are in keeping with the ship's overall theme and providing plenty for everyone to do whilst enjoying the sunshine. The two main pools are grouped together and have real teak wood for their surround and a hard-wearing imitation teak simulant on the floor that is decorated in a predominantly wood finish to reflect their natural environment. A water feature in the centre of the main arena becomes part of *Britannia*'s recently introduced deck show in the evenings where a combination of lights, colours and sound bring to life an area that is normally underused once it becomes dark. Twin

staircases lead up to the Sun Deck and the sports areas where there is a running track, sports court and some golf nets to practise in. As well as an array of sun loungers there is an excellent choice of quality food and beverages offered in one of the many nearby bars and restaurants including the Lido Grill, the Pizzeria and the new Grab and Go Counter serving a range of pre-packed snacks, sandwiches and salads. Whether a light, healthy bite or something more indulgent, passengers will find a range of freshly made pizzas, gourmet burgers, salads and sandwiches, all quickly and conveniently available whilst relaxing around the pool or simply enjoying their day in the sun.

In addition to the two main swimming pools there are four whirlpools and an additional swimming pool at the rear of the Lido Deck which has space for sun loungers built up like a small amphitheatre, with a waiter service bar and a seating area offering fantastic views over the ship's wake. Towards the front of the ship is the Serenity Pool and Bar where you will find the ship's third main pool surrounded by deeply padded beds and luxurious sun loungers, all designed to enhance your relaxation in a quieter part of the ship. Overlooking the bow of the ship is the Retreat, an al fresco spa terrace offering treatments under airy cabanas or simply a place to relax on padded sun loungers, huge outdoor beds and chairs that look like they would never let you back up the moment you sit down. And why would you have to with your own steward serving you cold drinks and a selection of fresh fruit and other fine foods as you absorb the panoramic ocean views? Put simply, the Retreat is the

*The decision to integrate **Britannia**'s artworks with its interior style has ensured a consistency of design and attention to detail that runs throughout the ship, creating a sophisticated, yet comfortable ambience. (P&O Cruises)*

Art on board ranges from paintings and bronze sculptures to ceramics and paper wall reliefs which have been created by a wide variety of artists – most of them British – with some from as far afield as Japan, Australia and South Africa. (P&O Cruises)

*Even the corridors on the **Britannia** have been designed to a very high standard and feature some of the 8000 pieces of art commissioned for the ship. (P&O Cruises)*

*At night the pool area has a completely different atmosphere and will be the setting for some unique entertainment designed exclusively for **Britannia**. (P&O Cruises)*

*As **Britannia** approaches the Ocean Terminal for the very first time, red white and blue confetti is launched in to the air, signifying the start of the week-long celebrations. (P&O Cruises)*

height of grown-up sophistication that provides a luxurious outdoor experience, described by some as a little bit of heaven at sea.

Britannia houses Britain's largest floating art collection, encompassing more than 8,000 pieces and representing an investment of several million pounds by P&O Cruises. Fine art consultant, Tom Tempest-Radford who has worked on many of P&O Cruises new ships over the years, was the adviser on the artworks that were to be displayed in the public areas. Rather than displaying pictures and sculptures simply to fit a space or a theme as an interior decorator might, Mr Tempest-Radford has sourced original artwork that is in complete harmony with the ship and provides a source of genuine interest and pleasure for the passengers. The collection draws on a pool of predominantly British artisans including painters, sculptors, ceramicists, textile artists, jewellers and goldsmiths whose work flows seamlessly throughout the ship. Most of the artworks are abstract in keeping with Britannia's contemporary theme and reflecting Britain's love of music and the sea. The majority of works displayed on the ship are from female artists, including a series of 18 dyed and hand-woven textile artworks called 'Beyond the Sea, A Homage to Blue' by Ptolemy Mann, 24 marble panels for the Horizon restaurant by Jemma Lewis and 64 large oil landscape paintings by Laura Rich for each of Britannia's Suites.

According to Mr Tempest-Radford, women are better at

producing surfaces and textures that have an incredible depth of flavour and Britannia has a huge variety of really crafted materials on display that will enrich the lives of people who are experiencing it. Located next to the Shore Excursions Desk are modern British icons such as Dr Who, The Queen, Mary Berry, Noel Gallagher, Monty Panesar, James Dyson and Bradley Wiggins as part of two unique pieces of art reflecting the 'Spirit of Modern Britain', produced by artist Johnny Bull.

Aboard Britannia, contemporary glamour is enjoying a renaissance. Her interiors are compelling and go beyond harsh functionalism into the realms of romance; they are contemporary and effortlessly elegant with a British flavour. With P&O Cruises offering a range of extended holidays, passengers have the time and leisure to appreciate the artwork on display throughout the public areas and in their cabins. Conversational pieces are interwoven with the best of modern British design and a subtle element of surprise co-exists in perfect harmony with the glamour of the sophisticated wows like the much-fabled 'Star Burst'. Her contemporary five star luxury makes her a modern classic and a ship worthy of her title as flagship of Britain's premier cruise line. Anything else just wouldn't be British.

*With her water cannons firing spectacularly over **Britannia**'s bow, the tug **Svitzer Alma** provides the traditional wet welcome for a new ship on her maiden call. (Andrew Cooke)*

Norwegian port of Flam as **Britannia** makes her maiden call there on 29th April 2015. (Tomas Ostberg Jacobsen)

BRITANNIA

Chapter Four

Meet Your P&O Cruise Crew

CAPTAIN PAUL BROWN

Country of Origin: United Kingdom
Joined P&O Cruises: 1989
Joined the Britannia: October 2013 as part of the newbuild team
Previous P&O Ships: Aurora, Artemis, Arcadia (both), Azura, Canberra, Oceana, Oriana, Victoria, Ventura

Captain Paul Brown knew at a very early age that he was going to have a career at sea as he was born in that famous sea port of Kingston upon Hull in East Yorkshire, where he attended the Hull Trinity House Navigational School at the tender age of 13. His desire to follow a career at sea was instigated by his fascination with the television series 'The Love Boat', which incidentally included P&O Cruises own *Victoria* as one of the ships used in the series. Just before taking his O Levels, Paul applied to the P&O Group for a cadetship hoping to work on one of their many tankers, ferries or even cruise ships. However, before he got a firm offer from the company he managed to secure for himself a job with BP Tankers as a Deck Cadet. In January 1982 he attended the South Shields Marine and Technical College where he started a four-year cadetship that would give him the experience needed to start his career at sea. Paul really enjoyed his work on the tankers but the one thing that the job did not give him was the opportunity to travel to a range of diverse destinations and to see different parts of the world. So in 1986 he transferred to the Royal Fleet Auxiliary where he worked on replenishment tankers, ammunition ships and landing craft learning his trade and finally getting to see a bit more of the world that he was hoping that his career would allow him to do. Paul remained with the Royal Fleet Auxiliary for another three years before he got the opportunity to join P&O Princess Cruises in the summer of 1989 and work on a completely different type of ship.

His first ship was the *Sea Princess* which he joined in Vancouver, Canada, and at 27,000 tonnes was to Paul a very enormous passenger ship indeed. He transferred to the then *Royal Princess*, which became the *Artemis* for P&O Cruises and so started his long association with his current employer. After a short spell on the *Royal Princess* he transferred to the *Canberra* and then the second ship in the P&O Cruises fleet to be called the *Arcadia* where he continued to work his way up the ranks until after 25 years at sea, he was finally promoted to the rank of Captain on the magnificent *Aurora* in 2007. Paul spent three years as Captain of the *Aurora* before moving to become the relief Captain on the new *Azura* in 2010 where he also served on her sister ship, the *Ventura*, before applying to be the Captain of the new *Britannia* in 2013.

When not working on *Britannia* Paul divides his time between homes in West Sussex and Javea, Spain where he likes to spend his spare time gardening.

DESCRIBE A TYPICAL DAY ON BOARD THE BRITANNIA.

It's difficult to outline a typical day on *Britannia* as it's

Captain Paul Brown. (Brian D. Smith)

quite true to say that no two days are ever the same. The main variation in my routines is brought about by the difference between a day at sea or a port day. On a sea day I will usually be called by the Bridge at around 07.00 to be given our overnight progress, the navigational situation and the predicted weather conditions for the day. I will also liaise with the Chief Engineer at an early stage to make sure that we have the engines configured in the most economical way so that we are using the optimum amount of fuel for our passage to the next port of call. Once I have readied myself for the day I will spend the first hour in my office catching up on emails and checking with the Operations Centre in Southampton to see if anything new or important has come up. I will also check my diary and prepare for the various meetings and events that are planned for the day.

By around 08.00 I am in a position to make my rounds of the ship. This starts by visiting the Bridge to check the navigational situation and progress towards our next port of call, along with confirming any times that may be relevant for our passage that day. Once I have satisfied myself that all is well, I then start a general walk round of the ship on my way to the Officers' Mess to get my breakfast. *Britannia* is of course a very large vessel and this can easily occupy a large amount of time depending on which areas I visit. I like to try and include areas such as the buffet where passengers will be enjoying breakfast as this also allows me to chat and say hello and answer the many questions that people like to ask me. After breakfast, I visit the many crew and

Captain Paul Brown receives a framed cast of the Royal Mint's new Britannia £2.00 coin from their Director of Commemorative Coins and Medals, Shane Bissett. (Christopher Ison)

operational areas around the ship and I will always make a point of calling in to see the Chief Engineer, the Deputy Captain and the Hotel General Manager to catch up on any issues that require a face-to-face discussion, and to understand what may be going on within their departments that day.

Once I have completed the walk round it is usually back to my office to start the various meetings that invariably are scheduled to take place on days at sea, or to commence some of the official ship inspections that are required on a regular basis. This includes things such as hygiene inspections, safety inspections and accommodation inspections and again these can take quite a lot of time to complete to a satisfactory standard. These inspections are important for the safe operation of the ship and we at P&O Cruises take all inspections very seriously indeed. After I tend to walk across the top of the ship on the open decks to speak with passengers and to get a feel for how things are going on a personal level. My morning will now usually be over and I will take a break for lunch.

I am often asked by passengers just how much time I spend on the Bridge. I have an extremely professional and competent team of Bridge Officers whom I can trust to navigate the ship whilst I am engaged in the numerous other duties that occupy my time, and I am always contactable and available to the Bridge Team at short notice by use of the pager system. Obviously, it varies significantly

depending on the navigational area and the current sea and weather conditions.

After a lunch break, it's back into my office as it is normally about this time that I carry out most of the administration-type tasks associated with the Captain's role. There will inevitably be e-mails from our Head Office to respond to, and reports to complete as well as the internal e-mail traffic that arises from the large on-board organisation. Quite a lot of this will also relate to personnel matters for which I have the assistance of another senior officer, our on-board Human Resources Manager. As you can imagine, with a workforce of over 1400, the sorts of issues that come to light can be many and varied and this is quite rightly an area of increased focus.

Before getting ready for any evening functions, I will make another brief visit to the Bridge, and then again before retiring, when I will write my Navigational Night Orders. This is a traditional means of formally passing on my requirements for our overnight passage to the current and incoming Officers of the Watch.

A day in port will be most notably different due to my duties in manoeuvring and berthing the ship. I will always be on the Bridge at least 30 minutes before we are scheduled to embark our local pilot and will then be actively involved in the navigation and handling of the ship. The local pilot rarely if ever actually manoeuvres the ship. The complexity of our equipment and the characteristics of the ship are

*Unmistakably the pride of the P&O Cruises fleet, **Britannia** returns to her builders after the successful completion of her sea trials at the end of 2014. (Fincantieri)*

such that we depend on his local knowledge and advice, but the bridge team maintains control of the ship. Where we are cruising to can also have a big factor in how my day pans out. For example, when we are cruising up in the Norwegian Fjords on a trip to say Olden, I start work at 03.00 as I have to be on the Bridge whilst we are navigating in the confined spaces of the Fjords. When we go to Flam, which includes a passage down the 116 nautical miles long Sognefjorden, I am on the Bridge from just after midnight. This can take around eight hours so once we arrive in port I will complete my obligations then sleep before the return passage later that evening. In contrast, when we are in the Caribbean we will be typically visiting nine ports during a two-week cruise so that can be a lot of early starts as we come in and out of the islands.

One of the aspects of my job that I love the most is that it is so varied, and therefore trying to outline a typical day is somewhat difficult, but this gives a good insight into a day on *Britannia* for the Captain. It is an intense and demanding job which gives me a great deal of pleasure to perform. Bringing *Britannia* into Southampton Water for the first time and being present when she was named by Her Majesty the Queen, were some of the proudest moments of my professional life and something that I will never forget. If you see me walking around the ship please feel free to come up and say hello; it will always be my greatest pleasure to speak to you.

CHIEF ENGINEER: SINCLAIR ROSS

Country of Origin: United Kingdom

Joined P&O Cruises: July 1989

Joined the Britannia: 13th January 2014 as part of the newbuild team

Previous P&O Ships: Adonia, Aurora, Arcadia (last and current), Canberra, Oriana

Sinclair Ross was born in the Scottish capital of Edinburgh to a large seafaring family who loved working in the maritime industry. His father and grandfather were both marine engineers who certainly had a big influence on Sinclair, so when he left school at 16 years old he went to the Maritime College in Aberdeen where he studied his cadetship, laying the foundations of what was to become a very rewarding career at sea. Two years later he got his first job on a ship called the *Benalbanach* with Ben Line Steamers based in Edinburgh before completing his cadetship at Glasgow's Nautical College. He then returned to Ben Lines to work on the Benreoch, a semi-submersible exploration rig out in the North Sea where he worked mainly as a control room operator, much like a current Senior Engineer Officer of the watch on *Britannia*. Having spent several harsh winters out in the depths of the North Sea, Sinclair decided to join Shell Tankers as a Junior Engineer where he was assigned a ship called the *Serenia*, before moving to the very large crude carrier, *Lampas*, the biggest ship Sinclair has ever sailed on with a displacement weight of over 315,000 tonnes when fully loaded. He later

worked on the gas carrier *Bubuk* before applying directly to P&O Princess Cruises in 1989 for the post of Assistant Engineering Officer on the *Canberra*. Since then, Sinclair has worked on various ships of the P&O Cruises fleet before achieving the rank of Chief Engineer on their current *Arcadia* back in 2006.

When away from *Britannia* Sinclair lives in the village of Knowle in the West Midlands with his partner Bernadette and her two daughters where he likes nothing more than spending time with his family and looking after his collection of fine motor cycles.

DESCRIBE A TYPICAL DAY ON BOARD THE BRITANNIA.

My day rarely starts at the same time as I will be called by the Engine Control Room for "stand by" around 30 minutes before we arrive in port. The Chief Engineer, or Staff Chief Engineer, has to be present in the Engine Control Room whilst the ship is under stand by conditions like the Captain has to be on the Bridge. It is very important at the start of each day to make sure I know what has happened during the night. Due to weather conditions we may have had to speed the ship up to avoid any unnecessary high seas which can give the passengers an uncomfortable ride or to keep to our designated itinerary if we have been delayed for any reason. There could also be a technical issue with either the machinery or the hotel area of the ship which might require resolving quickly early on in the day, especially if this will affect any of the passenger services. On a sea day

Chief Engineer Sinclair Ross. (Brian D. Smith)

*The Engineering Officers of **Britannia** in one of her main engine rooms. (Sinclair Ross collection)*

we start at 07.00 so I will start the day with a walk around the accommodation to get a feel for how things are going and to see if there are any maintenance issues that have not yet been raised.

Once we have arrived safely in port, I will come into my office to check my e-mails before holding a morning meeting with my team to discuss any issues from the previous night, the day ahead and any planned maintenance that is due to be carried out. Once this is completed I like to walk through the engine room and engineering spaces to observe how things are going and to talk to some of the staff about issues that might not have yet been raised. Due to the size of the engine room I find that I have to focus on certain compartments each day or else you could spend the whole day just in the engine room, so about 11.00 I try and make it back to my office.

As *Britannia* is a brand new ship I have to make sure that I keep an eye on the guarantee items that are currently under warranty with the shipyard. At the moment we have two guarantee engineers currently travelling with us from P&O and Fincantieri and I have to liaise with them to make sure that any of the major items of equipment that are guaranteed by the builders are functioning correctly and that there are no concerns around their performance. There are numerous administrative duties that I am required to complete and one of the most important are the fuel logs depicting our daily fuel consumption. I have to monitor how much fuel we have on board and how much the next planned bunkering is going to require. The fuel is the most

expensive aspect of our operation and optimum performance is very important to make sure that we don't waste fuel unnecessarily. Today's marine engines are very fuel efficient compared to those being built only a few years ago and *Britannia* has the most efficient engines in the P&O Cruises fleet.

After lunch I will try and have an hour's rest before checking in again with my department to see how things are going. In the afternoon I find myself back in the office doing administrative tasks mainly ensuring compliance, computerised maintenance, itinerary fuel planning, personnel issues and dialogue with the Southampton office. I also like to keep in touch with the Captain and various department heads to ensure we have a smooth operation.

When the ship is in port I have to attend the Navigation Bridge at least 30 minutes prior to departure where the Captain holds a briefing on the planned manoeuvre from that port and we agree what engine configuration is best and the most economical for the passage. Once we are clear of the port and out into the open sea I can look forward to one of the more pleasurable aspects of my job which are the opportunities to attend some of the important social events we hold here on *Britannia* such as the Captain's Welcome Onboard Party. Another of my favourites are the Peninsular Club lunches, which are held for our most loyal passengers. During these social events, people like to ask me all sorts of questions about the ship and it is important that I am able to answer their questions, even if they are not within my sphere of operations. Meeting and interacting with the passengers is a very enjoyable part of the job and something I appreciate very much.

As Chief Engineer I have a very close liaison with my Technical Stores Manager on board to monitor our maintenance costs and what is being ordered for the ship. As *Britannia* is so new she does not need a lot of new parts and most of the equipment we order is for the routine running of the vessel. As Chief Engineer I work closely with the Environmental Compliance Officer to make sure that we are complying with the very strict environmental regulations that apply to any discharge of waste products from the ship. It is all part of the responsibilities for being in charge of the technical department of such a wonderful ship and I consider myself very privileged indeed to have achieved the rank of Chief Engineer with a company such as P&O Cruises and to serve them on a ship like *Britannia* is something for which I am very grateful indeed.

EXECUTIVE CHEF: DARREN DEEGAN

Country of Origin: Ireland
Joined P&O Cruises: April 1998
Joined the Britannia: May 2015
Previous P&O Ships: Adonia, Arcadia, Aurora, Azura, Oceana,
Oriana, Ventura

Darren Deegan grew up in the picturesque market town of Ballymote which is situated in County Sligo, Ireland. It is a historic town with the magnificent Ballymote Castle, the last and the mightiest of the Norman "keepless" castles in Connacht, and also the home town of Brother Walfrid, the founder of the famous Glasgow Celtic Football Club. His father was a Chef in the Royal Navy so naturally Darren developed an interest in cooking so when he left school he enrolled at the Killybegs Tourism College in County Donegal on a two-year apprenticeship studying Hospitality & Tourism which lead to a City & Guilds qualification in cookery. Once qualified Darren got his first job with a company called Manor House Hotels at the Ballincar House Hotel (now known as the Sligo Park Hotel) as a Chef Tournant.

Two years later Darren left his home country to travel to London where he got himself a job as a Commis Chef at the Cumberland Hotel in Marble Arch. It was whilst working in London that Darren saw an advert for an opening with Cunard Line so, deciding that this could be a chance to follow in his father's footsteps he applied, but was regrettably turned down because of his youthful looks. Unperturbed, Darren applied for the position of First Commis Chef on board the new *Oriana* for P&O Cruises. He was also known as the Diet Chef as he was responsible for preparing the menus for all the passengers with specific requirements such as wheat intolerance or an allergy to a specific food group. As he says with a smile on his face, "I came for one contract and stayed for 20 years!" P&O have clearly enjoyed working with Darren and liked what he has done for their passengers as in 2012 they promoted him to Executive Chef on board the *Oceana*.

It is fair to say that Darren's life has been shaped by the sea as not only did his father work for the Navy but so does

Executive Chef Darren Deegan. (Brian D. Smith)

his fiancée Cheryl who was working on board the *Ventura* as a Wine Steward when they first met back in 2012. When not working on *Britannia* Darren lives in the Philippines where he likes to spend his spare time looking after his young son Caelan and running two business, one dealing with office and school supplies and the other in the music industry.

DESCRIBE A TYPICAL DAY ON BOARD THE BRITANNIA.

My day starts when I head to my office to check the overnight e-mails and any other business that has come my way overnight. I then walk around *Britannia*'s 18 different galleys to speak with the night staff before they go off duty. I will always speak with the Night Duty Sous Chef to discuss the previous night's preparations and any challenges that were faced. As most of the day staff have now started work I am able to talk to practically all of the 194 chefs that we have here on *Britannia* during my walk around. This also gives me the opportunity to meet up with some of our passengers who like to stop for a chat, especially those who recognise me from one of the other ships in the P&O Cruises fleet that I have worked on.

Then I will chair a meeting with the Inventory Manager and the Senior Food and Beverage Team to discuss the previous day's business and to find out what went well and why. We also look to see if anything unforeseen came up that we could have been better prepared for so that it does not happen again. We then go through the next two days' menus for all of the restaurants to make sure that we have the correct products available and are not going to unexpectedly run out of anything. This gives us an opportunity to make any necessary changes at an early stage. Here I will approve the food requisitions, making sure that it is delivered to the right galley at the right time and that I have authorised enough to cover the 16,000 meals we would expect to serve in a 24-hour period on board the ship.

Once this is completed, I will meet with the Food and Beverage Manager to discuss the individual needs of each restaurant's daily requirements and whether we need to be flexible around opening times to accommodate passengers who have gone ashore and are on an extended tour or excursion.

By now most of the restaurants will have finished serving breakfast and I will host a tasting table with the Chef De Cuisine and the Sous Chefs. This is where we taste the lunch menus, making sure that it is of a perfect flavour, taste and presentation suitable to be served according to the recipes and menus expected of P&O Cruises. This gives us the opportunity to correct any imperfections and make any necessary alterations so that the food we serve is to a consistently very high standard and presented just as we would like it to be to our passengers and fellow crew members.

Before lunch is served, the Chef De Cuisine and I will inspect the inventory stores with the Inventory Manager to make sure that our fresh produce such as the vegetables, fruit and cheese are being properly rotated and we are not going to run out before our next replenishment. Hopefully this will all be completed before I head up to the Horizon Restaurant to make sure everything is set up for lunch and give a quick briefing to the Chef De Cuisine and their team.

Once lunch is successfully underway throughout the ship I will have something to eat myself before carrying out some of my other daily duties such as planning future menus, overseeing any function's that might be coming up like the Peninsular Club lunches or making arrangements for the Celebrity Chefs that we have up in the Cookery Club.

We have a break before the main part of the day which of course is the evening meal. Every restaurant on *Britannia* is open in the evening including the three main restaurants and the premium restaurants which may have not been open for lunch or breakfast which makes this time of the day a little intense. We again hold a tasting menu for all our restaurants to make sure that the food we are preparing is still prepared to our specifications and tastes. This involves a lot of walking around on a ship as big as *Britannia* and certainly helps me to stay in shape when I am surrounded by so much tempting food throughout the day. Again I will walk to each venue to speak in person with the Chef De Cuisine and their team and check the product before serving starts.

During the evening meal I will be on hand to offer advice and support wherever and whenever it is required and to help sort out any unexpected issues that occasionally arise. I have a good team here on *Britannia* and most evenings everything runs like a well-oiled machine. Dinner

is the highlight of the day for many of our passengers and it gives me great satisfaction to see so many happy people when I walk around the public areas knowing that they have just had a great dinner service and are clearly enjoying their cruise.

Once the dinner service is completed, I will hold a briefing with my team to discuss the evening's performance and to see if the amount of food that we used was as we expected before supervising the cleaning of the entire operation and that everything is properly put away and isolated before finishing my day's work. Normally at this time I will relax and Skype with family.

COOKERY CLUB MANAGER: LIZZIE KENNEDY

Country of Origin: Northern Ireland
Joined P&O Cruises: January 2015
Joined the Britannia: February 2015

Lizzie Kennedy is a proud lady from Northern Ireland who talks very fondly of where she lives. This is her first job with P&O Cruises and, in fact, this is her first job at sea in what can only be described as an extremely varied and exciting career. She joined *Britannia* in February 2015 when she flew out to the shipyard where she was being built to help set up the Cookery Club and was part of the team who brought the ship back to Southampton. She played an

Two ladies of great distinction, Lizzie Kennedy and Mary Berry.
(P&O Cruises)

Lizzie Kennedy's warmth and friendly personality are a major contribution to the success of the Cookery Club. (P&O Cruises)

important role in the inaugural celebrations and was present when the ship was named by the Queen a few days later.

Lizzie is part of an Irish family that grew up in Warwickshire where, upon leaving school, she applied for a commission into the British Army, where her claim to fame is that she was the first female officer to command male soldiers. During her time in active service, Lizzie was attached to the Royal Engineers and the Royal Signals, serving both at home and abroad where she became an Adjutant and a trainer before meeting her husband and moving to Germany for five years. When Lizzie returned to the UK she had two children to look after so she joined the Territorials as a Captain before being offered a role as a Catering Officer. As an Army Officer's wife, Lizzie had a lot of experience in entertaining distinguished guests so this was a natural progression and when you consider that an army marches on its stomach, you can see how important this role can be.

When Lizzie returned to civilian life, she moved to Washington DC where she was again involved in professional entertainment. Looking after Diplomats and other important people, she got the opportunity to further improve her culinary skills before moving back to the UK and enrolling in the highly respected Tante Marie Culinary College in Surrey. Her natural flare for cooking earned her the top student award whilst studying for her Cordon Bleu diploma, giving her the confidence to open up a cookery

school of her own in Northern Ireland, after undertaking what she describes as an eclectic range of different jobs that you would expect from someone who has travelled around the world.

Since then, Lizzie has moved back to the United States where she was involved in an IT company before returning to Northern Ireland and resuming her cookery school. It was during this time that she was approached to see if she would be interested in applying for position as Head of the Cookery Club on *Britannia*, alongside colleague Rob Cottam.

DESCRIBE A TYPICAL DAY ON BOARD THE BRITANNIA.

A day in the Cookery Club does depend if we have one of the Food Heroes working with us on board. If it is a sea day there will be two classes whilst if it is a day in port then we will usually only run one class in the afternoon. This gives the passengers the opportunity to visit the port then come back on board for a cooking lesson. On an average two-week cruise we will run up to 19 different classes, each with its own theme lasting for around two and a half hours. They are aimed at people with all levels of ability and we do our very best to make it a fun and enjoyable thing as I do understand that some passengers who are not confident in the kitchen may be a bit apprehensive, but I make sure that everyone is welcome.

I have a team of two chefs from the main galley and an assistant working alongside me. We have 12 stations for 24 people working in pairs and an area especially designed to make it easier for wheelchair users to join in. At the start of the day we come up to the club around 08.00 and set up the equipment that we are going to need ready for the first class. If we have a full sea day then we will have done much of the preparation the night before so we get a head start. As the actual teacher of the class I am responsible for the delivery of the class and also making sure that we have enough ingredients that the students will be using during the lesson and depending on the type of lesson that I am teaching that can include numerous different ingredients. These ingredients have to be set out at the workstations so that when the passengers arrive, everything is laid out in front of them ready for them to start cooking. This can be very challenging and it can take around three hours to get the club ready for the first lesson.

When the passengers arrive I personally greet them and give a short health and safety briefing as this is a working kitchen and I need to know that everyone is aware of the risks involved in such an environment. I like to get started straight away as we usually prepare three different dishes throughout the class. Sometimes we will do any extra dish or I will demonstrate one or two dishes, it depends on the class and what we are trying to achieve. The classes have all been carefully designed to include ingredients that are easy to find as we want the passengers to recreate the dishes when they are at home. Many of the themes reflect the regions that we are visiting during the cruise. Whatever happens, I make sure that everyone is enjoying themselves and at the end of the day everyone gets to eat everything that has been cooked at the specially designed Chef's Table. After the class, the chefs and I will do all of the clearing up as we do not expect the passengers to be doing the washing up after the lesson has finished.

When we have a Food Hero on board then it is slightly different. We will have one or two classes, depending if it is a sea day, and have a hosted dinner in the evening here in the club. This involves me liaising with the chefs whilst they are still ashore to make sure that I have everything that they require when they come on board so that they can deliver a masterclass without any worries or concerns. I become the assistant helping both the Food Hero and the passengers throughout the day. In the evening, the Food Hero will cook for 16 passengers, which is a real treat for those lucky enough to get a place as these dinners book up well in advance. They come up to the club in the dress of the day and are greeted with a pre-dinner drink and often some canapes whilst at the same time watching the chef physically preparing their meals. They then sit down to have a wonderful time which simply cannot be matched anywhere else in the world, with the Chef hosting the table. This is a wonderful experience for the passengers and we make sure that their every desire is met whilst they are enjoying themselves. Once the event is completed my staff and I will clean the kitchen down and get everything ready for the next day.

In my opinion the Cookery Club on *Britannia* is the most impressive cookery school in the world. It is a purpose-built, state-of-the-art feature with every conceivable amenity that you need to prepare any meal that you desire. Some of the equipment in here is so wonderful that it just takes your breath away. When you combine that with the incredible views that you get from being 17 decks up then you get an idea of what the club is all about. I mean how good is life when you can have your dinner cooked by Marco Pierre White or James Martin whilst you watch the sun setting behind Venice or one of the Norwegian Fjords with a glass of fine wine in your hand. Every day is an absolute joy to work in and I love every minute of it. Come and see me when you are sailing on *Britannia*. You won't be disappointed.

ENTERTAINMENT MANAGER: NEIL OLIVER

Country of Origin: United Kingdom
Joined P&O Cruises: July 1991
Joined the Britannia: November 2014
Previous P&O Ships: Adonia, Aurora, Arcadia (2nd and 3rd),
Azura, Canberra, Oceana, Oriana, Victoria, Ventura

Neil Oliver was one of eight children born into a large family in the county of Essex. At the tender age of four years old he was placed into a dance school every Saturday morning with one of his sisters whilst their mother went shopping. It was the beginning of a lifelong interest in entertainment which continued when he left school to become a professional dancer, where he was performing in many shows in London and around Europe. He also became a regular on the original BBC 'Come Dancing' series. In early 1991, Neil was working in a partnership when they received a call from P&O Princess Cruises asking if they would be interested in working on one of their ships as dance instructors and performing some cabaret in the evening. Both of them jumped at the chance and began work on the *Sea Princess* for Princess Cruises which became the *Victoria* for P&O Cruises. The company clearly liked what Neil and his partner were doing because at the end of the year they offered them a contract to sail with the *Sea Princess* on her world cruise. In the end they stayed with the company for a further four years sailing all over the world and enjoying Caribbean seasons throughout the winter months.

It is fair to say that 1995 was a year of transition for Neil as after nearly ten years working together, Neil and his dance partner decided to go their separate ways with Neil being offered the role of Entertainments Officer on the *Canberra*.

Neil showed a lot of dedication and passion for his passengers and continued to work his way up the ranks to the position of Assistant Cruise Director and then finally Cruise Director when in 2000 he was chosen to lead the Entertainments Team on the recently transferred *Star Princess* from Princess Cruises which had been renamed the *Arcadia*. After a short spell on the *Arcadia*, Neil transferred to the *Aurora* whilst she was still being built in Germany and helped bring the ship into service during her inaugural

*Neil Oliver has been the Entertainment Manager on every new P&O Cruises ship since the **Aurora**. (P&O Cruises)*

season. Since then Neil has been chosen to lead the Entertainments Team on every new P&O Cruises ship, cumulating in the magnificent *Britannia* on which he is serving today.

When not on the ship, Neil lives in West Sussex and Spain where he enjoys nothing more than his life in the country.

DESCRIBE A TYPICAL DAY ON BOARD THE BRITANNIA.

Being responsible for all the entertainment on the ship means that a sea day is the big event for me as I have to make sure that all the planned entertainment runs smoothly and that everyone gets the opportunity to appreciate whatever it is that they have chosen to enjoy. On these days I will get up early and start the day in my office going through my e-mails and completing all the clerical work that needs to be completed before the day really gets going. I then walk around the ship. You get to know the regular passengers and they are always happy to give me feedback which I find very useful and I do act upon, as at the end of the day, we want nothing more than to give everyone the perfect holiday. Sea days are prime time to meet the passengers as we are together for the whole day and I believe that it is the best way to get an honest reflection of what we are doing.

As Entertainment Manager, I attend the Operations Meeting which we hold on the first sea day of every cruise where all the heads of Departments from the different teams get together with the Captain. After this meeting I will hold a conference with my own entertainment team where we discuss what our operation is going to include for the current cruise. This can be very important if we are having a themed cruise, like one of the 'Strictly Come Dancing' cruises as this will be very popular with the passengers and we have to be very ingenious in the way that we allow everyone who wants to see the performances get to enjoy the shows. We have to plan the entertainment very carefully to make sure there is enough going on to satisfy everyone and nothing important clashes, which will leave some people disappointed. Some events are simply so popular that we cannot allow everyone who would like to see a show access to the venue so then I have to make it a ticketed event and we will discuss how we are going to make those tickets available to the people who desire them the most. We might also have our Health and Safety meeting or our Activity Schedule meeting where we are formulating for our future cruises as we are always looking ahead to see what we can plan for the passengers and how we go about arranging that entertainment.

One thing that the British love is light entertainment. When you see what we watch on television such as 'Deal or no Deal' or 'Who Wants to Be a Millionaire?' then you can appreciate what is popular on the ships. We organise all sorts of game shows, quizzes, karaoke and of course the ever popular bingo sessions which are very much cherished by the passengers and always fill the venues that they are being held in. On trips to places like the Norwegian Fjords, the Crow's Nest bar is very popular throughout the day. I monitor this to make sure that there is something programmed to help people enjoy the occasion. We have an excellent cocktail pianist on board and people love listening to live music. On such cruises I will arrange for additional live music to be played at venues such as this by moving it from somewhere that is not so in demand. It is all about watching what is going on around the ship and being flexible to meet people's needs.

By the time evening comes around, I will get changed for one of the many functions that we hold here on *Britannia* such as the Cocktail Nights or the Welcome Onboard party. I will also host the productions shows that *Britannia* Show Cast are performing in the theatre and guest cabaret show. In between performances I can be found interacting with passengers around the public areas. I will visit the other entertainment venues to see how the shows, tribute acts and musicians are doing. At the end of the evening I will collate all the feedback about every act that has performed on the ship so that I can do an end of voyage report covering all aspects of the entertainment including the Youth Team as I am responsible for them as well.

On a port day life on board still goes on but it is not so intense for me during the early part of the day. I still have to provide entertainment for the passengers who decide to remain on the ship and with a ship like *Britannia*, which has an abundance of facilities to enjoy, then that can mean several hundred people who choose to remain on board. We have the very popular Sail Away parties on the open

*Light Emitting Diodes provide the backdrop to the Britannia Theatre Company as they perform one of many new productions especially written for **Britannia**. (P&O Cruises)*

decks when we leave port and I have to make sure that my team are prepared for this and have what they need to put on a good show. Likewise, for the Great British Sail Away when we have the decks all decked out in British bunting and the passengers get lots of British flags to wave. Most of the Entertainment Team will be up on deck for that as they can be a high-energy event which requires a lot of input from everyone and I have to make sure that everything runs smoothly.

After, it is back to the evening job and my work is pretty similar to that of a sea day with shows in the theatre and the different acts performing all around the ship. It's all part of the Entertainment Manager's responsibility and I love every minute of it.

Normally my day finishes around midnight when I will usually check for any last minute emails before unwinding and going to bed.

HOTEL GENERAL MANAGER: DALJIT SHARMA

Country of Origin: India
Joined P&O Cruises: November 2010
Joined the Britannia: January 2015
Previous P&O Ships: Arcadia, Azura, Oceana, Ventura

Daljit Sharma was born in the Northern Indian town of Shimla where he grew up with his Uncle, who was a Commander in the Indian Navy in the picturesque Andaman & Nicobar Islands. This would involve a seven-day cruise or ferry passage back across the Bay of Bengal to Madras when he wanted to go home. When Daljit finished his education he travelled to Mumbai and enrolled in one of India's famous Hotel Schools gaining the necessary experience and qualifications to start a career in the hospitality industry. Having grown up in a naval family he always had an interest in ships and everything nautical so in 1990 he applied to Carnival Cruise Lines and was given the post of Assistant Food and Beverage Manager on board the TSS *Festivale*.

The following year Daljit was one of ten lucky crew members chosen by the company to attend the prestigious Austrian Hotel School in Salzburg where he studied Maritime Hotel Management before returning to Carnival Cruise Line for a further seven years working on ships such as the *Celebration* and the *Fantasy*, reaching the position of Food and Beverage Manager.

By this time, most of Daljit's career had been spent sailing out of the United States so in 1997 he decided to apply for a role with V Ships based in Monaco, where he was based on the Seawing. A few years later Daljit decided

Hotel General Manager Daljit Sharma. (Brian D. Smith)

to move to a company called Airtour Sun Cruises before returning to the United States and working for Premier Cruise Lines who were the official cruise line of Disney at that time. Regrettably, shortly after, the company applied for bankruptcy so Daljit again moved employers to Renaissance Cruises working out of Tahiti where he was finally promoted to the rank of Chief Purser. Once fully promoted, Daljit joined Thompson Cruises and then Ocean Village Cruises, which of course brought him back under the Carnival Corporation umbrella. When Carnival decided to end the Ocean Village brand, Daljit joined his current employer and moved to the P&O Cruises brand in 2008 working on the *Ventura*, the *Oceana* and the *Arcadia* before being selected as part of the team to bring the *Azura* into service in 2010. After a successful transition period on the ship he was selected to be the Hotel General Manager on *Britannia* and again bring a ship into service directly from her builders.

During his time away from the ship Daljit lives in Delhi where he likes to go mountaineering, hiking and on long drives in the countryside.

DESCRIBE A TYPICAL DAY ON BOARD THE BRITANNIA.

One thing that I am, is mobile. I believe that you can achieve so much more by moving around and talking to people than by just sitting at a desk and sending e-mails. The Captain and the Chief Engineer both know that the best

way to get my attention is to phone me and not send an e-mail. On a ship you are never more than 200 metres from anybody and I can soon get to speak with whomever I need to speak to and have a face-to-face conversation which is much more personal and far more productive.

Holding a senior position on a passenger ship is very different from working on a cargo ship. When you are on a cargo ship you lash the cargo down at the start of the voyage and that is it. On my ship, the cargo is very precious and walks about so you have to plan your day to look after it very carefully indeed. The first thing I will do when I start my day is talk to the Night Duty Manager, as he is my representative during the night. He will give me a briefing as to what has happened and identify any issues that need to be brought to my attention. I then go and liaise with the Customer Services Manager to see if there are any passenger complaints that are still outstanding or need my personal intervention. Then it's off to the Finance Manager to see how the relevant revenue streams performed before speaking with what I call my four hotel seniors, the Food and Beverage Manager, the Hotel and Retail Manager, the Entertainments Manager and the Housekeeping Manager. Here I will identify any challenges that they have and what their plans for the day are, especially any distinct events or if any high-profile people are coming on board that require additional consideration. Once I have finished all these meetings then I go and speak with the ship's Senior Doctor to see how things are in the Medical Centre.

By now it is late morning and I will begin a walk around the ship to see how the passenger flows are going and speak with the rest of the crew. It is also an excellent time to talk to our passengers and find out how they are enjoying their holiday. By doing this, I like to think that I have a very good idea of what is going on for both the crew and the passengers so nothing should come as a surprise to me later in the day.

At lunchtime I will go down to the Officers' Mess for something to eat or I might eat in one of the passenger restaurants if I am interacting with someone and it has become a social occasion. This is something I very much enjoy and take great pride from. As far as I am concerned my entire responsibility is to give the passengers the perfect holiday. If there is anything that I can do to make them enjoy themselves even more then I will do it. Keeping the passengers happy is what it is all about. I have a saying that if you help the passengers then they will remember you and if you don't help the passengers then they will still remember you, but for the wrong reasons. This can never be allowed to happen.

In the afternoon I will catch up with my administrative duties and make plans for the evening and night-time events. Once these are under way, I do like to watch a show in the theatre or one of the acts going on around the ship to get a feel for how the passengers appreciate what we are doing. I finish around 23.00 when I will take a final round of the entertainment venues and the Horizon late night buffet before retiring for the day.

I have been working at sea now for 25 years and I am extremely privileged to be working for such an established company with so many delightful people and serving on

The Sindhu Bar. (P&O Cruises)

Excursions Manager Marian Weldon. (Brian D. Smith)

Britannia is a dream come true. If you see me walking around when you are on board please come and tell me about your day as it will be my absolute pleasure to talk to you.

EXCURSIONS MANAGER: MARIAN WELDON

Country of Origin: United Kingdom
Joined P&O Cruises: June 1995
Joined the Britannia: February 2015
Previous P&O Ships: Adonia (1st and current), Arcadia (2nd and 3rd), Aurora, Azura, Oceana, Oriana, Ventura and Victoria

Marian Weldon hails from the north west of England being born in Bolton and growing up in the small town of Little Hulton. After she left school, her first job was as a Secretary for a political party, which she found interesting but not inspirational. One thing Marian did enjoy were her holidays to warmer climates so it did not take her long to realise that what she really wanted was a life in the travel trade.

Whilst on one of her many holidays she became friendly with a number of the Holiday Representatives that worked for the big tour companies and when she was 24 years of age she managed to get a job working in the Greek Islands as a Rep, which also gave her the added bonus of working in the Gambia during the winter months. She enjoyed this so much that she remained in Greece for

11 years becoming a Resort Manager where she would spend the winter season back in the UK recruiting and training new Reps ready for their life in the sun.

When her company was merged with another travel company, Marian decided that it was time for a change so she went to work for a company called Trans Global Vacations looking after passengers for Chandris Cruise lines on the Amerikanis and their ship called the *Victoria*. Her responsibilities made her the company's Holiday Representative but she would also book and arrange shore excursions for passengers and deal with any administrative and logistical problems that occurred. Marian did this for one winter season in the Caribbean before returning to her original employer as a Resort Manager for the following summer season. This was the pattern of her life for another year or two until she applied for the job of Shore Excursions Manager with P&O Cruises in 1995.

After a successful interview, she was appointed to another ship called the *Victoria* and so started her long and successful career with the company. Since that time she has served on all of P&O Cruises current fleet, including one or two that are no longer with us and is now responsible for the shore excursions on the largest and most impressive ship she has ever worked on.

When at home, Marian likes to spend time with her family and friends, travelling to destinations that are unavailable when working on a cruise ship. She has a house on the beautiful island of Crete where she enjoys relaxing and immersing herself in the Greek way of life.

DESCRIBE A TYPICAL DAY ON BOARD THE BRITANNIA.

Being a Shore Excursions Manager on *Britannia* is very different from any other ship in the P&O Cruises fleet, or any other ship that I have worked on come to that. *Britannia* is all about giving passengers choice and from a shore excursions point of view we can offer an unrivalled choice of places to see and visit at every port of call. New multimedia technology on board *Britannia* has enabled us to really enhance the way we advertise and allow passengers to book their excursions. This is the first ship in the fleet where the shore excursions area offers interactive kiosks where passengers can browse and book the many excursions on offer. This allows my team to move around the area and offer our help and advice as it is needed. It is a far more personal service than simply talking to people across a desk showing them brochures as you might see in a high street travel agents. It also means that passengers can book their tours at a time to suit them, as the kiosks are available 24 hours a day.

My team consists of three Assistants and a Port Presenter who gives live talks on board about our ports of call. For all of us a day in port is an exciting day where we will get up early to make sure that the shore excursion desk is staffed just in case anyone has any last minute questions or wants to see if there are still places available on the excursions. If we have a lot of people going off on tour then we need to control the flow of passengers leaving the ship. In this instance we often arrange for one of the ship's lounges to be used as a meeting place. Two of my staff remain in the lounge whilst an assistant and I go ashore to liaise with the coach operators, brief the guides and generally manage the logistics of getting everyone on their tours safely and on time.

On a port day the entire shore excursions team will be assigned an excursion that they will accompany so that we can increase our knowledge of the tours that we are offering. This is very important when future passengers come to ask questions as we have first-hand knowledge of the shore excursions and can share our experiences. It also allows us to monitor the guides and how they interact with the passengers, check the quality of the transport and generally make sure that the tour operator is providing the high-quality product that we have contracted them to provide.

When we return to the ship I always make sure that the shore excursions area is open so passengers can feed back their experiences – we love to hear how the excursions have gone. We normally close the shore excursions office around 19.00 then make sure that all the arrangements for the next port are complete before calling it a day. Then we will grab something to eat and spend some time with our friends and contact family back in the UK.

On a sea day the shore excursions area is open all day so that passengers can come and visit us at any time for advice and recommendations on how to spend their time ashore. All of the team are available, but as the Manager, I start by checking the department's e-mails and arranging the day's schedule for everyone. I will also make sure that the preparations needed for the next port's excursions are completed. If there are any outstanding concerns then I will liaise with the Hotel General Manager or Port Agent to rectify these well in advance. We run a very slick operation and most of the difficulties that might occur ashore can be foreseen and dealt with long before they become an issue. Again the desk will normally close around 19.00 before we all finish for the day.

I have been working for P&O Cruises now for 20 years and working on *Britannia* is the pinnacle of my career with the Company. This is a fabulous ship with some remarkable facilities and I have a wonderful team working with me.

HOUSEKEEPING MANAGER: FITZGERALD RODRIGUES

Country of Origin: India
Joined P&O Cruises: October 1997
Joined the Britannia: January 2015
Previous P&O Ships: The current and original Adonia, Arcadia, Aurora, Azura, Oceana, Oriana, Victoria and Ventura

Fitzgerald Rodrigues comes from the famous Indian state of Goa on the Arabian Sea, where he grew up in a family of three brothers and got his first job working in a Holiday Inn Hotel as a Front Office Manager. He enjoyed working in the hospitality industry but wanted to see more of the world than where he grew up so, when one of his colleagues got a position with P&O Cruises he decided to apply directly with them. He was absolutely thrilled to be offered the position of Deck Manger on their new *Oriana*.

Housekeeping Manager Fitzgerald Rodrigues. (Brian D. Smith)

He remained with the ship for some time before being promoted to Housekeeping Manager in 2004 on the *Oriana*. Since then he has served on all of the company's current fleet, finishing up on the *Adonia* in 2012 before finally joining *Britannia* just before she was delivered by her builders in early 2015.

Fitzgerald still lives in Goa with his wife and two children whom he loves very much and looks forward to spending as much time with them as possible when he is not working on the ship.

DESCRIBE A TYPICAL DAY ON BOARD THE BRITANNIA.

My routine on board *Britannia* is very similar most days but there are slight differences between a turnaround day and any other day. This is because on turnaround day we have to cater for several thousand passengers leaving and boarding the ship in a short period of time which needs to be well managed and we all start a little earlier than normal. I basically start my day at 07.00 by speaking with our Night Housekeeper to see how things went throughout the night and to make sure that there is nothing outstanding that needs my urgent attention. Together we will then do a round of all the public rooms, a bit like walking round the Parish really, before going up onto the open decks to make sure that the Retreat and the pool areas are set up for our passengers and the items like the sun loungers, tables and other occasional furniture are all being set out correctly.

Once I am satisfied that everything is as it should be I will head down to my office to complete my clerical obligations and read my e-mails. I will then liaise with my assistant and set out our priorities for the day.

When these have been agreed I will head over to the main laundry area which is the focal point of our operation, as most of what we do emanates from this very important area. Here I will meet with other managers and members of my team where we discuss the issues of the day and any outstanding problems that we are working on. Here we have a new "Tunnel Washer" which is an industrial laundry machine designed specifically to handle heavy loads. It is a first for P&O Cruises and reduces the amount of water that we use in the daily wash cycle but we are still learning how to get the best from it so I keep an eye on how it is performing. I will also take time to visit the crew areas because on a ship of this magnitude, the crew area is quite substantial and we have a lot of staff dedicated to this procedure alone.

With responsibility for over 2,000 cabins on the ship, I have a department of around 230 personnel which means apart from supervising the work that they do, I also have to arrange their training, manage their leave requests and make sure that everyone knows their job as well as that day's responsibilities. So once I have finished doing my rounds I will return to the office to carry out my daily housekeeping duties which can be very challenging depending on what scenario I am dealing with. I will also look at any query that has come in and make sure that it has been dealt with to the satisfaction of the passenger. We

work very hard here on *Britannia* to give everyone the best possible holiday and nothing is ever too much trouble when it comes to looking after our guests.

By now it's time for lunch and I will take some time to get something to eat before wandering ashore for an hour or two if it is a port day or heading back to my cabin for a break if it is a sea day. I do try to make sure that I get a few hours' rest in the afternoon as this tends to be the quietest part of the day before I get myself ready for the evening session. This begins with another walk around the public areas to make sure that everything is in place and to get a feel for how the passengers are enjoying themselves on board.

Occasionally I have the pleasure of attending one of the cocktail parties before dining in one of the main passenger restaurants which helps me interact with passengers and get a feel for how they are enjoying the cruise. I always enjoy telling them about myself and what I do but the best bit is always telling them how much I love working for P&O Cruises. Before I break off for the day, I will have a quick meeting with the supervisors where they will bring to my attention any new problems that may have arisen. Then I pop into the laundry which is still going strong and will keep going right throughout the night. The last thing I do before signing off for the day is to check my e-mails and make sure that all the evening's tasks have been correctly assigned to the relevant personnel. Once this is done I get a chance to enjoy a meal with my colleagues and to unwind and relax in the Officers' Mess. Then it's off to bed for the start of another day.

Britannia is seen at the very top of Southampton Water in March 2015. (Darren Holdaway)

A very powerful view of **Britannia**
as she follows **Azura** out of their
home port towards the
Mediterranean. (Brian D. Smith)

BRITANNIA

SOUTHAMPTON

*The Irish sea port of Cobh has a long tradition of welcoming great British passenger ships to her shores and **Britannia** is seen on her maiden call during the summer of 2015. (P&O Cruises)*

PRINCIPAL PARTICULARS BRITANNIA

Builders:	Fincantieri, Monfalcone
Yard Number:	6231
Gross tonnage:	143,730 registered tonnes
Contract Price:	£473 million
Length overall:	330.00m
Length BP:	306.07m
Moulded Breadth:	38.38m
Breadth Overall:	44.00m
Design Draught:	8.30m
Maximum Draught:	8.55m
Air draught:	68.30m
Maximum Height:	76.60m
Displacement:	68,155 tonnes
Passenger Capacity:	3,647
Passenger Capacity, Maximum:	4,324
Number of Decks:	17
Crew:	1,398
Propulsion System:	Diesel-electric
Main Engine Power:	62,400kW
Main Generators:	2 x 14,400kW + 2 x 16,800kW
Main Alternators:	2 x 18,000kVA + 2 x 21,000kVA
Propulsion Motors: 3	6,000kW
Thrusters:	6 x 2,500kW
Speed: Abt.	23 knots
Class:	Lloyd's Register
Cabins:	1,837
Including:	64 suites, 1,313 balcony cabins including 15 single balcony cabins, 460 inside cabins including 12 single cabins
Contract Signed:	2nd June 2011
Steel Cut:	8th October 2012
Keel Laid:	15th May 2013
Float Up:	14th February 2014
Sea Trials:	6th December – 11th December 2014
Acceptance Date:	22nd February 2015
Naming Ceremony:	10th March 2015
Godmother:	Her Majesty Queen Elizabeth II
Call sign:	2HHG5
IMO number:	9614036
MMSI number:	235106595
Maiden Voyage:	14th March 2015
First Captain:	Paul Brown
First Chief Engineer:	Sinclair Ross

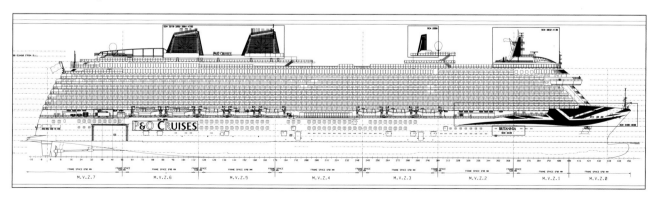

ACKNOWLEDGEMENTS

The author would like to thank David Dingle, the Chief Executive Officer of Carnival UK for agreeing to write the Foreword for this book and also express his sincerest gratitude to the very amiable Christopher Edgington, the Vice President of Marketing for P&O Cruises who has repeatedly given up his valuable time to help with many requests in compiling this book. A mention must also be made to Terry McGillicuddy from Richmond who spent many an hour going over the design concepts for *Britannia* with me and for allowing the use of his company's presentations in this book. I would also like to give a special thanks to Michelle Woodman and Samantha Cameron from P&O Cruises for their assistance and help with my numerous requests for all sorts of information associated with this project. Thanks must also go to David Pickett, the Head of Carnival UK's Newbuilding Division, who gave me permission to visit *Britannia* whilst she was being built. The joy of watching a cruise ship develop from keel laying to naming ceremony is something very special to me and I am very grateful to David and his team for the hospitality they displayed during my many visits.

From the Italian shipyard of Fincantieri, Efisio Piras deserves a mention for sharing with me his time and expertise and allowing his staff to show me round the ship during her construction. Another special thank you must go to the wonderful Lucia Racaniello, who knows more about painting than any other person I know and regularly gave up her time to escort me round the shipyard, no matter what the weather.

I would also like to thank Miles Cowsill of Ferry Publications who has done a magnificent job putting together yet another wonderful publication to add to his diverse library of superior maritime books. No other maritime publisher has such an in-depth knowledge of the industry and I am very grateful to him for allowing me to write my third book on P&O Cruises ships.

Finally, I must mention Captain Brown and the crew of *Britannia* who were so very welcoming on every occasion that I visited them, both on busy turnaround days in Southampton and whilst the ship was at sea. They are an extremely hard working group of talented people who are dedicated to providing their passengers with the best cruise experience possible and I hope I have done justice in conveying the extremely high standards they set for themselves.

*A magnificent ariel photo of **Britannia** at speed in the Adriatic Sea. (Fincantieri)*